The Exceptional Team Blueprint

A practical approach to building high performing teams and developing exceptional team members and leaders

Andrew Deighton
Chartered FCIPD

The Exceptional Team Blueprint™

Karin,

Hope you find this useful.

Best wishes,

Andrew

Contents

I owe a huge debt of gratitude to everyone who has helped, advised and supported me whilst I set up AWD Development Solutions Ltd., and to those who continue to do so.

Thanks to those who took the time to answer my request for help and who contributed and provided their thoughts, practical insights and their experiences of building high performing teams and on what makes a great leader. You've helped me to validate the Exceptional Team Blueprint.

Thanks to you for buying the book. I hope you find it useful, work through the activities and make progress on developing exceptional teams in your business, your organisation or your personal life.

But most of all, thank you to Jo, Hannah, Emily and Tom for your on-going patience and support as I moved from the relative financial stability of corporate life to the uncertainty, excitement, challenge and continuous development opportunities of running your own business.

Family is the ultimate team.

Introduction

The Exceptional Team Blueprint™ described in this book is a practical approach to building and developing a high performing team. It will help new, and established, team leaders become more effective at leading and developing their team. It will help owners of small businesses to improve the performance of their organisation by taking a broad-based approach to the development of their leaders and their employees. It will help leaders of departments and divisions in larger corporations and those bringing together a new team to deliver a specific project.

Teams don't need to be in a business environment to benefit from the Exceptional Team Blueprint. Applying the tools and techniques to teams based in the education, charity and voluntary sectors will bring positive benefits. You can also use the elements and apply the approaches with the teams you're a member of in your hobbies and interests.

You don't have to be in a leadership position to affect the performance of a team. You can positively influence how the team you're part of works and performs, and the outcomes it delivers, from the inside as a team member as well. Apply the elements of this Blueprint at a personal level to become a more effective team member.

The Exceptional Team Blueprint covers areas that I've found to be particularly useful from my personal experience and professional expertise. I set up my own people development business after a successful 26-year career with a FTSE 100 company. In my corporate working life I progressed from a graduate engineer position into senior roles in Employee Development and Human Resources.

Throughout my career I've been involved with many teams. My first role after university was as a team member designing compressor components for jet engines. I had to make sure that the design of the component I was working on was ready in time for it to be manufactured in order to meet the engine testing dates.

I've been the Human Resources (HR) team leader on a multi-disciplined project team tasked with building a £40m factory from a green field to a production facility in two years.

I was the HR Director on an executive team based in Singapore leading a business with 2,000 employees in 34 global locations. There I led a team of HR professionals based in four different countries from the USA to Asia.

I led a team of over fifty people who were responsible for the recruitment and development of apprentices and graduates in a blue-chip organisation. At any point we looked after approximately 2,000 trainees across the global business.

I've led a strategic workstream as part of a three-company joint venture team bidding for a £7bn civil nuclear decommissioning project.

Outside of work I've been involved with teams as a school governor and on the Board of Trustees of a charity. I'm a volunteer with the 'Inspiring the Future' organisation and I mentor university students.

I think there are several key essentials that need to be in place to produce exceptional team performance. You need exceptional team members working in an exceptional team environment, led by exceptional team leaders who create exceptional team spirit, operating within an exceptional team framework.

The Exceptional Team Blueprint provides that framework.

This book describes the elements of the Exceptional Team Blueprint in detail. It also covers some wider aspects around teams. It takes you through a series of explanations, practical activities, processes and steps. I've included some implementation ideas and suggestions, and tools and techniques to help you build exceptional teams and develop exceptional team members and leaders.

I don't think any of this should be over-complicated. I've kept things as pragmatic as possible to guide you through the various aspects, tools and activities. There's some white space in this book, which is deliberate. Use that space to answer the questions and complete the activities. Capture your thoughts and develop your ideas so you can develop yourself and the teams you're part of, or lead. This will ultimately help you to build success and grow your business or your organisation.

Why build exceptional teams?

Firstly, we should consider why we need to spend time building exceptional teams at all.

I've taken findings from research on the benefits of building high performing teams from a number of sources and summarised some of the key ones below. These sources include the University of Phoenix, Gallup, HerdWisdom, ClearCompany, ACAS and Room to Escape.

Over 70% of survey respondents reported that they were part of a dysfunctional team in their work situation. So there appears to be plenty of opportunity for improvement.

Ensuring that employees are engaged in their work has significant benefits. People who use their strengths on a daily basis are shown to be six times more engaged with their work. They are also 87% less likely to be looking to change roles or leave the business. Allowing for recruitment costs, management time, training costs and reduced productivity, the estimated average cost of replacing a single employee is £30,000. Therefore, reducing employee turnover can save a significant amount of money.

Research found that highly engaged teams are 22% more productive on average than teams that are not engaged. That's an extra day in a typical five-day week.

A lack of alignment and direction was said to negatively impact team performance and outcomes by 97% of people surveyed. However, only 14% businesses said their employees understand the strategy and direction.

A lack of communication and poor collaboration was reported to have a negative effect on team outcomes and cause failure by 86% of respondents.

Poorly led or managed teams were found to be on average 50% less productive and 44% less profitable than teams that are reported to be well led or managed.

So the benefits of improving performance at both an individual and team level appear to be very strong.

Building exceptional teams in a business or organisation will help to provide

- improved focus and delivery,
- improved team relationships,
- more capable and engaged team members, and
- reduced team member turnover and absence.

In turn, those improvements should lead to

- improved efficiency and effectiveness,
- improved team performance,
- improved financial performance, and ultimately
- improved business results and growth potential.

Therefore, I think there's a strong case for us all to aim to be better team members and better team leaders so we can build and be part of exceptional teams.

Types of team

There are many different types of team and team situations that you might be involved in. It may be that you're part of several teams at the same time. You could be a team member in one team and in a leadership role in another.

In a workplace environment, potential types of team could include

- Work-based teams who are together on an on-going, day-to-day basis
- A project team that has a defined life cycle and specific end point
- A team of supervisors, managers or leaders in a larger organisation
- A senior management or executive leadership team
- A start-up team in a new business
- All the employees in a small business
- A remote or virtual team with internationally-based members

Outside a workplace environment, potential teams could be

- A team of volunteers on a committee
- The Board of Trustees of a charity
- The governing body of a school or college
- A Parent Teacher Association (PTA) for a school
- A sports team
- Your family

These are not exhaustive lists, but illustrate some potential team situations that you may find yourself in.

I think the fundamental principles of building an exceptional team, and developing the team members and leaders, are the same regardless of the team type or the situation. However, it's likely that some areas of the Exceptional Team Blueprint will have greater or lesser focus and relevance than other areas. This will depend on the circumstances of the team.

As you move through the areas of the Blueprint you will need to prioritise the areas that your team really needs to focus on. This will ensure that you spend your time and resources on the areas that will have the biggest impact. In turn, this will produce the largest benefits to the team and its performance.

My Plans, Reflections, Ideas, Next steps and Thoughts

As you work through the Blueprint, use the 'PRINT' approach to capture some actions and to help yourself commit to delivering those actions.

Plans – what are my plans and goals around this area?

Reflections – what do I think about what I've read?

Ideas – what new ideas has this triggered for me?

Next steps – what actions do I need to take now?

Thoughts – does anything else come to mind?

Exceptional Team Blueprint overview

The Exceptional Team Blueprint™ is built up of elements and areas that I've found to be particularly important and valuable. These are collated from my personal experiences as a team member in many different teams, and as a team leader of several teams. The Blueprint also incorporates ideas based on my professional knowledge. Above all, I wanted to produce a framework that is practical and pragmatic. I wanted it to be easy to apply and adapt to a wide range of businesses and organisations, across a wide range of situations.

The Exceptional Team Blueprint is backed up by research. I sought input from owners and leaders of successful businesses and organisations of differing size, and from individuals with specialist knowledge. The Blueprint is structured in a way that allows you to focus on different levels of detail to make it as easy to use as possible and relevant to your particular situation.

The top level of the Exceptional Team Blueprint consists of four elements.

1. Purpose – *why* the team exists.
2. People – *who* is in the team.
3. Processes – *how* the team operates.
4. Performance – *what* the team does.

These four elements form the core of the Exceptional Team Blueprint and are shown in Figure 1.

Purpose	People
Why the team exists	*Who* is in the team
Processes	**Performance**
How the team operates	*What* the team does

Figure 1. Top level elements of the Exceptional Team Blueprint™

1. Purpose.

The starting point for building and developing an exceptional team is to have a clear purpose around why the team is together. Members of the team need to understand, clarify and review why the team exists. They must then make it meaningful to themselves at a personal level.

2. People.

Teams are made up of people. In order to build and develop those individuals into an exceptional team it's essential that there's an in depth understanding of who is in the team. This should be from both a personal perspective and from a role perspective.

3. Processes.

How the team operates from a practical perspective is the third key element for building an exceptional team. Defining and creating an understanding of the processes that the team uses on a day-to-day basis will help to get the work done as effectively and efficiently as possible.

4. Performance.

Finally, you need to manage the team's performance. You must ensure you're making the most efficient and effective use of the team members and their resources and making the progress you'd expect. It's important that the leader knows how things are going and that the team members know how things are going. The performance should link back to the team's purpose.

Each of the four high level elements of the Exceptional Team Blueprint breaks down into four further sub-areas. This allows more focused and detailed work and development to be carried out.

The sixteen areas are given below. They are shown in Figure 2 and will be explored and discussed in detail throughout the book.

Purpose
- Challenge and deliverables
- Vision
- Values
- Commitment and alignment

People
- Structure and roles
- Styles and preferences
- Skills and capabilities
- Standards and behaviours

Processes
- Ways of working
- Learning and knowledge
- Improvements
- Support

Performance
- Goals
- Planning
- Measuring
- Reporting

Purpose		People	
Challenge & Deliverables	Vision	Structure & Roles	Styles & Preferences
Values	Commitment & Alignment	Skills & Capabilities	Standards & Behaviours
Processes		Performance	
Ways of Working	Learning & Knowledge	Goals	Planning
Improvements	Support	Measuring	Reporting

Figure 2. The sixteen sub-areas of the Exceptional Team Blueprint™

The Exceptional Team Blueprint is relevant to all types of organisations across all sectors. It can be deployed in businesses, education establishments, charities, public sector organisations, and in the voluntary sector. It can also be used in organisations of any size. To simplify things, I use the term 'business' throughout the book, but mean all the above.

The book covers the four top level elements and the sixteen sub-areas in detail. It then considers some of the wider aspects that support the building of an exceptional team and developing highly effective team members and leaders.

My Plans, Reflections, Ideas, Next steps and Thoughts

Purpose

"The team must understand why they are doing what you are asking them to do."
David Hyner, Stretch Development

The purpose of the team forms its fundamental core and is the foundation on which all other activities are built. Creating a detailed understanding of why the team exists will help to generate team performance and success. It will enhance and exploit the strengths of the people in the team.

I was talking with the Corporate Fundraiser from a local hospice at a networking event and it really got me thinking about the importance of having a clear purpose for a team. The hospice's extremely powerful purpose statement is given below.

"To make every day count through giving the highest quality support for patients and families living with life limiting illness or affected by death and dying"

That's an amazingly powerful and motivating purpose for the staff and volunteers at the hospice to have. The team members see and experience their purpose, first hand, every day. That really gives meaning to their work and provides them with the motivation for everything they do.

Identifying the challenges that the team has to address, and the deliverables it has to meet are the starting points for working on the team's purpose at a deeper level. Setting a clear vision based on the purpose, and defining a strong set of values generates alignment and commitment within, and across, team members. This provides motivation and direction to the team members, and engages them.

The team can then develop a strategy of how to move towards their vision, meet their challenges and deliverables, and ultimately achieve success. The strategy and the approach that the team takes may well change over time, as the environment in which the team operates changes. However, the purpose, vision and values of the team are likely to remain consistent.

If the team members know what they're aiming for, and why they're doing it, their activities and actions will be much more focused, integrated and cost effective.

Working through the four areas of Challenges and deliverables, Vision, Values, and Commitment and alignment in detail will provide a solid foundation for building the team's success.

Challenges and deliverables

"Build effective teams that understand their role within the organisation. Putting real context to the team's contribution within the charity's overall aims and mission is a must."
Paul Naylor, Direct Help & Advice

Defining the challenges that the team has to address, and the deliverables the team is required to achieve gives team members a clear focus. It helps members understand why the team that they are part of exists. Teams will go through difficult times and low points. Having an understanding of the challenges and deliverables can provide individual team members with the motivation to keep going and keep driving forwards.

Gathering team members together to discuss the challenges and deliverables will start to build a shared understanding and create shared ownership.

Work through the following questions as a team and capture your responses.

> Why are we together? Why does our team exist?

What is our team's purpose?

What are our customers' requirements? What do our customers expect?

What specification requirements have we been given?

What are our team's main deliverables?

What challenges do the team have to solve?

What problems or opportunities are we addressing?

What main tasks must we accomplish to achieve our purpose?

My Plans, Reflections, Ideas, Next steps and Thoughts

Vision

"The most important thing about building a team is to have a shared vision. It is also important that people feel they can feed into that shared vision as an equal."
Sharon Stevens-Cash, Gravity Digital

Once the team has identified why it exists, it can move on to developing its vision. Pick a time in the future and think where the team wants to be. Think of this as the team's ultimate big picture and big goal.

If there is a time frame for the team to achieve its deliverables, then the end of that timeframe should be the point of the vision.

If the team is an on-going, work-based team without a specific timeframe of deliverables, or end date, then think sufficiently far ahead to give time to work towards the vision.

Create the vision in a way that works for the team members. Write down what you'll see, hear, feel and smell when you achieve your vision. Use words, images and phrases from newspapers or magazines. Produce a mindmap. Draw a picture that represents the vision.

In whatever way you capture it, make the vision real to the team members.

What is the team's ultimate big goal?

Where does the team ultimately want to be?

What words and phrases describe the team's vision?

What images represent the vision for the team? Draw a picture that represents the team's vision.

Capture a summary of the vision that the team develops.

Now produce a simple vision statement which is engaging and motivational to the team members.

My Plans, Reflections, Ideas, Next steps and Thoughts

Values

> *"I feel we all get much more enjoyment out of our jobs if we are invested in the values of the work and why we do it."*
> **Rob Twells, Frogspark**

Values are the things that are most important to you from a personal and business perspective. They guide your behaviour and choices. They form the basis of your decisions. In general, values will be stable and consistent, but they may evolve during periods of significant change.

Values underpin how the team operates, how team members treat each other and how they treat their customers. If you align team members and their challenges, work tasks and personal development with a strong set of values then they'll feel much more engaged, energised and fulfilled.

Identifying a set of shared values for the team can be difficult to do, but the following process will help to achieve it.

Ask team members to work through the process from an individual perspective initially. The team can then look to develop a set of shared values.

Step 1.

Think about the following questions from a personal, education, work or career perspective and capture some specific examples.

When were you happiest and what were you doing?

When did you feel most proud and what had you done?

When did you feel most motivated, inspired, energised and fulfilled and what were you doing?

What is really important to you?

What drives you?

What do you really enjoy?

Step 2.

Based on your thoughts and the examples you captured in Step 1, think of the underlying reasons why you felt that way and the words you used when you answered the questions.

Build a list of values that link to these reasons and words, and are important to you. Use the list of values given on pages 42 to 44 to prompt your thoughts. Limit yourself to an initial list of about ten values.

Step 3.

Prioritise your values to your top three. If you struggle to decide between two values, compare them and think about each. Which one you would choose if only one of them could be satisfied?

1.

2.

3.

Step 4.

For each of your top three values, write a short description of what success means for you if that value is satisfied.

1.

2.

3.

Step 5.

Review each of your top three values and statements of success. Think whether they make you feel good and do they make you feel proud?

If not, rethink and reconsider your list and repeat the process

Step 6.

Share the individual team members' values and discuss them to begin to collate a set of shared team values.

Build an initial list of no more than ten team values.

Step 7.

Prioritise the shared team values to the top three.

1.

2.

3.

Step 8.

For each of your top three shared team values, write a short description of what success means if that value is satisfied.

1.

2.

3.

Some values

Ability	Challenge	Delivery
Abundance	Charity	Dependability
Accountability	Clarity	Depth
Accuracy	Commitment	Desire
Achievement	Community	Determination
Adaptability	Compassion	Devotion
Adventure	Competence	Dignity
Affluence	Competition	Diligence
Altruism	Composure	Diplomacy
Ambition	Concentration	Direction
Appreciation	Confidence	Directness
Approachability	Conformity	Discretion
Assertiveness	Connection	Discipline
Attractiveness	Consciousness	Discovery
Availability	Consistency	Diversity
Awareness	Contribution	Drive
Balance	Control	Duty
Being the best	Conviction	Dynamism
Belonging	Cooperation	Eagerness
Boldness	Correctness	Education
Bravery	Courage	Effectiveness
Brilliance	Courtesy	Efficiency
Camaraderie	Creativity	Elegance
Capability	Credibility	Empathy
Care	Curiosity	Endurance
Certainty	Decisiveness	Energy

Enjoyment	Growth	Kindness
Enlightenment	Guidance	Leadership
Enthusiasm	Happiness	Learning
Equality	Hard work	Legacy
Excellence	Harmony	Logic
Excitement	Health	Longevity
Exhilaration	Helpfulness	Loyalty
Experience	Helping society	Mastery
Expertise	Heroism	Maturity
Exploration	Honesty	Mindfulness
Expressiveness	Honour	Moderation
Exuberance	Imagination	Motivation
Facilitating	Impact	Openness
Fairness	Impartiality	Optimism
Family	Improvement	Order
Fascination	Independence	Organisation
Fearlessness	Ingenuity	Originality
Finesse	Inner harmony	Passion
Firmness	Inquisitiveness	Perfection
Fitness	Insightfulness	Perseverance
Flexibility	Inspiration	Persuasiveness
Focus	Integrity	Philanthropy
Frankness	Intelligence	Playfulness
Freedom	Intensity	Pleasantness
Friendliness	Intimacy	Pleasure
Fun	Introversion	Popularity
Generosity	Intuition	Positivity
Giving	Inventiveness	Practicality
Gratitude	Justice	Pragmatism

Precision	Restraint	Smartness
Presence	Results focus	Sophistication
Privacy	Rigour	Solidarity
Proactivity	Satisfaction	Solitude
Productivity	Security	Speed
Proficiency	Self-fulfilment	Spirituality
Professionalism	Self-control	Spontaneity
Prosperity	Selflessness	Stability
Punctuality	Self-realisation	Strategic
Quality focus	Self-reliance	Strength
Realism	Sensitivity	Structure
Recognition	Service	Success
Refinement	Sharing	Sufficiency
Reflection	Shrewdness	Support
Relaxation	Significance	Teamwork
Reliability	Silence	Thoughtfulness
Resilience	Simplicity	Timeliness
Resolve	Sincerity	Tolerance
Respect	Skilfulness	

My Plans, Reflections, Ideas, Next steps and Thoughts

Commitment and alignment

"You need a clear understanding of the purpose of the team and how it fits into the rest of the organisation. This includes how the team goals link to overall business strategy and how each individual's objectives and role contributes to the team."
Diz Lamb, Ardagh Group

Gaining the commitment of team members and their alignment to the team, its purpose, vision, values and to fellow team members is another critical aspect of building an exceptional team.

Team members must feel that they belong to something that really matters to them so that they engage with it. Commitment and alignment provides and builds focus. Buying in to a common purpose and vision, linked to a set of shared values can give the motivation to go on when things get tough. It helps team members through the low points because they understand 'why' the team is doing what it's doing. It's particularly effective if team members can link why the team exists, and why they are a member of that team, to their own personal situation and circumstances. This generates real meaning to them.

Individual team members will have their own motivations and reasons for being part of the team. They will also have their own views on what the success of the team will mean for them at a personal level.

Work through these questions at an individual level.

What does being a member of this team mean to me
and why do I want to be a part of it?

How will being part of this team benefit me from a
professional or career perspective?

How will being part of this team benefit me from a personal perspective?

How will being a member of this team help me with the things that are important to me?

Next, work through the following questions as a team. This will help to build understanding, alignment and commitment, and create a shared ownership within team members for the success of the team.

What are our team's top five business priorities?
1.
2.
3.
4.
5.

What are our team's top five people priorities?

1.

2.

3.

4.

5.

What might stop us achieving our priorities as a team?

How can we overcome those barriers?

What are our expectations of the level of commitment of team members to the team?

How will the team and its members benefit when the vision is achieved?

Another technique that can help bring a vision to life for team members, and create strong alignment and commitment, is to write an 'affirmation'. Affirmations are descriptions of what you want, or need, to achieve. They can help to give real focus and motivation. Writing an affirmation based on what it will be like when the team achieves its vision brings that vision to life. It makes the vision real to the team members and gives them an emotional connection. This helps to motivate team members towards achieving it.

Use these points to help write an effective team affirmation.

- Write it in the first person – use "We" or "I".
- Write it in the present tense – e.g. "It's 21st June 2023 and we are...."
- Create a positive picture (achieving the vision).
- Build a specific and detailed picture.
- Use different senses in the picture you build to get a strong emotional connection.
- You must believe that you can achieve it.

Write a team level affirmation for the vision.

As well as creating an affirmation at the team level, team members should create an individual affirmation. This affirmation must be relevant and personal to them. It will help to focus the team member on how achieving the vision will have a positive impact on them, and what's important to them.

The Exceptional Team Blueprint™

Ask individual team members to write their own personal affirmation.

Purpose – A personal example

The importance of having a clear purpose became very clear to me several years ago. I was the HR team leader on a multi-disciplinary project implementation team. Our challenge was to deliver a new manufacturing facility from a green field site and in to production in a two-year timescale. The total investment by the business in the project was £40m and it would incorporate new technology and new HR approaches.

It was my first HR position and there was a blank sheet of paper for much of the HR aspects. There would be new terms and conditions, new shift patterns, a new reward strategy, new career structures, new recruitment approaches, new induction and training methods, self-managed teams. The list went on.

As part of my role I had to brief the affected employee population and explain the changes that were being introduced from an HR perspective. Because the existing employees worked a three shift system I had to deliver 24 identical one-hour briefings over a 48 hour period to cover everyone as quickly as possible.

Probably the lowest point in my career happened when I was briefing one of the night shift teams. It was about 2am and I'd already delivered around half of the planned sessions. The previous briefings had gone as well as could have been expected given the sensitivities of what was being implemented. But in this session the environment suddenly changed. It became very hostile, very threatening and very unpleasant.

I got through the briefing and as I was driving home at around 3am I asked myself "Why am I doing this? Why am I putting my family and myself potentially at risk?" It really was that unpleasant. I nearly gave up. It was the closest I've come to quitting anything.

I went into the office the following morning and talked the situation through with the Project Manager. From the launch of the team he'd been clear that we needed to define why we were working on the project, and the difference it would make. He encouraged us to do this at a business level as a project team and also at a personal level as individual team members.

There was a very clear business case purpose for the project. This focused on the usual aspects of improving product cost, quality, manufacturing lead-time through the facility and customer satisfaction.

At a personal level I saw this as a once-in-a-career opportunity to be involved in a new facility build. It was a chance to do something that would influence the company going forward. It gave the opportunity for me to develop new skills within a new function. This would potentially lead to career progression which would, in turn, positively benefit my family.

Reminding myself of the purpose and why I wanted to be involved at a personal level in the project gave me the focus and motivation to keep going. I did carry on, and delivered the HR aspects of the project within the required timescales to meet the project plan.

Purpose - Key learning points

- The purpose of the team is its fundamental core and foundation. It's why the team exists.
- The team's strategy and approach may change over time depending on circumstances, but the team's purpose should remain consistent.

Challenges and deliverables

- Be clear on the challenges the team has to address.
- Define the key deliverables the team has to achieve.
- Understanding the challenges and deliverables gives the team focus.
- Build shared team member understanding and ownership.

Vision

- Pick a time in the future and define the team's ultimate big picture and big goal.
- Identify words and phrases that define the team's vision.
- Produce images that represent the vision.
- Capture the vision in a way that makes it real to team members.
- Produce a simple vision statement which is engaging and motivational.

Values

- Values underpin how the team operates. They guide behaviours and choices, and form the basis of decisions.
- Team members who are aligned to a shared set of values are more engaged, fulfilled and energised.
- Help team members to identify their personal values.
- Facilitate the development of a set of shared team values.

Commitment and alignment

- Help team members to feel that they belong to something that really matters to them.
- Understand how being part of the team will benefit each member from an individual personal, professional and career perspective.
- Define the expected level of commitment to the team.
- Produce a team affirmation to assist team members in creating focus and motivation to deliver the vision.
- Produce individual team member affirmations that are personal, relevant and meaningful to them.

My Plans, Reflections, Ideas, Next steps and Thoughts

People

"Selecting a team is all about the mixture of abilities, personalities and differing contributions, and ensuring everyone recognises what their contribution should be."
Bev Crighton, University of Derby

"There's no I in team" is one of those clichés that you listen out for in business if you're sitting in a boring meeting and playing management speak bingo. But in reality, all teams are made up of people. Each of those people is an individual, and each of those individuals has their own drivers and motivations.

In order to build and develop an exceptional team it's essential that there's an in depth understanding of who the members are. This understanding needs to cover the skills and capabilities of the team members as well as their working styles and preferences.

The team members need to be structured in an effective way, with clarity around their individual roles and responsibilities.

The standards and behaviours expected of team members must also be clearly defined, communicated and bought into.

Structure and roles

"It's important to have clarity of individual roles and responsibilities."
Julie Broad, Rolls-Royce

Whenever possible, the way the team is structured should be considered. If it's a new team that's being formed then this can be relatively straight forward. You can structure the team from a blank sheet because nothing exists. If it's an established team then the structure should be assessed at an appropriate time. As the team grows, the structure should be regularly reviewed to ensure that it's supporting the operation of the team in the most effective and efficient way.

Once you have a team structure outline you'll need to consider the detail of the roles needed in the structure. You should capture the responsibilities of the roles, as well as the skills, knowledge, behaviours and experiences required to perform the roles successfully.

Structuring your team

Fundamentally, your team structure defines how the work is divided up between team members. This should be such that work can be carried out as effectively and efficiently as possible. When your team is small it's likely that you'll want a high degree of flexibility around what people do. The larger your team gets, the more important it is to have real clarity and differentiation between the roles team members have, and their individual responsibilities.

If your team already has a structure, then you should start with a review of how things currently work within that structure.

Consider these questions.

What does the team have to deliver?

What are the main activities that the team has to perform in order to deliver?

What works well in the current structure?

What are the issues with the current structure?

How does the current team structure have a positive or negative impact on its customers?

Positive

Negative

What are the costs of operating the current structure?

Are there any overlaps of responsibility and activity between different roles in the structure?

Are the team members clear about the current structure and how it operates?

Do the team members have any ideas about how the current structure could be improved?

How should the work be divided up across the roles?

How much flexibility do we need between the roles?

How permanent is the team?

Is the team structure 'future proof?'

Once you've reviewed the existing structure you can then begin to consider the ideal team structure.

There are a number of options as to how to structure the team. Each option will have pros and cons for your specific situation. These will depend on the size of the business, the size of the team, what the team's purpose is and what its challenges and deliverables are.

A few generic structural options are;

- Product or service based
- Geographically based
- Customer based
- Functionally based
- Process based
- Matrix

Product or service based structure

In a product or service based structure, teams are organised around the business's product or service offerings. Each team carries out all the functions and activities needed to produce and deliver a particular product or service.

Geographically based structure

In a geographically based structure, teams are organised around the specific geographic regions that they serve. For example, within the UK teams could cover the north of England, the south, Scotland, Wales and so on. In larger businesses with export markets, some teams may cover Europe, and beyond, such as Asia Pacific, the Americas and Africa.

Customer based structure

In a customer based structure, teams are organised around specific customer types. This may be customers such as domestic or corporate, or in specific sectors such as health, professional services, logistics, etc.

Functionally based structure

In a functionally based structure, teams are organised according to the technical or professional function that they perform. For example, functions could be Sales, Design, Production, Finance, Marketing and HR.

Process based structure

In a process based structure, teams are organised in a way that cuts across the vertical functions. The team will include people who can carry out all the activities in a particular business process. A single team carries out the whole process from start to finish.

Matrix structure

As the size of a business grows, a matrix structure might be appropriate. In this structure the business may want to exploit the benefits of teams focused on a particular project but also maintain the technical expertise of functional departments. This could mean that employees have two (or more) bosses.

In reality, it may be that team and business structures are hybrids. There could, for legitimate reasons, be a mixture of structural forms within the organisation.

To identify and design the ideal team structure you need to consider the team's purpose, challenges and deliverables. Does the purpose affect how the team may need to be structured in the future? Depending on the permanence of the team, if you don't future-proof the structure it may be that you'll have to revisit the design of the structure as you start to implement and deliver the team's or business's purpose. This would result in wasted time and money. Also, you might not have recruited the right people for where the team is going, and needs to go, in the future.

You may be able to eliminate some potential structural options very quickly, but there might still be a number of options that could work. Produce a decision matrix to compare and score the potential options relative to each other. An example matrix is shown in Figure 3.

	Option 1	Option 2	Option 3
Pros			
Cons			
Overhead cost estimates			
Other relevant criteria...			
Total score			

Figure 3. Team structural options decision matrix

Once you've identified the preferred team structure, you can move on to a more detailed level of design thinking.

Consider the roles needed within the structure. This falls into two parts. Firstly, think about the purpose, key responsibilities and work that will be done by each role. Make sure there is a clear differentiation between what the different role types do. Ensure there's no overlap in responsibilities between role types. Secondly, consider how many people you need in each role type. Depending on the size of the team, and the nature of the work, you could have several people doing the same type of role.

The number of team members required may mean that you have to split them into sub teams and allocate some supervisory, management or leadership positions. When considering the supervisory structure of a team, one concept to bear in mind is that of 'spans and layers'.

The span of a role in a structure refers to the number of direct reports into that position. If the span is too small (i.e. a small number of direct reports) then it may be that you are employing too many managers or team leaders. This adds unnecessary cost to the business. If the span is too great (i.e. a large number of direct reports), it may be difficult for one individual to manage the wide variety of reports from both a time and capability perspective.

The number of layers in a structure refers to the levels of hierarchy. For example, in a large team the Project Director of the team is 'layer 1', their leadership team of direct reports is 'layer 2', and the individual team members are 'layer 3'.

There should be as few layers of management and supervision as practically possible between the most senior team role and the individual team members. This speeds up decision-making and communication, and enhances team member engagement. This is often referred to as a 'flat' team structure.

There's no perfect answer to the number of spans and layers in a team structure. It depends on aspects such as the purpose of the team, its size, its complexity, its likely growth, the nature of the work, the capability of the team members, and the nature of the leader. However, some best practice suggests that a target should be a span of around eight to ten direct reports and a maximum of three layers within the team.

Defining the roles in the team

Once you've got your team structure defined and some high level thoughts about the responsibilities for the roles within the structure you can move on to the detailed role definitions. You should produce simple and clear role profiles for each position.

Whilst the roles may be interdependent, it's important that there are no overlaps or duplications of accountabilities between them. If there aren't clear differentiations then there is likely to be confusion and lack of focus across the team. This in turn will reduce the efficiency and effectiveness of how the work is done.

The role profiles will form the basis of team member recruitment and selection, development and performance management (appraisal) activity.

A role profile should contain the following elements:

- Role title
- Reporting line for the role
- Role purpose
- Key accountabilities
- Key behavioural competencies required (Essential and desirable)
- Key experiences required (Essential and desirable)
- Knowledge required (Essential and desirable)
- Education and qualifications required (Essential and desirable)
- Key relationships that interface with the role
- Key performance indicators

Wherever possible, keep a role profile to a maximum of two A4 pages. However, this will depend on the level and complexity of the role.

An example role profile template is given on page 75.

Role title:

Reports to:

Purpose
• A simple, high level statement which says why the role exists

Key accountabilities
• A list of the key accountabilities of the role • This must not be a list of day-to-day tasks

Key behavioural competences required
• What are the 'Essential' and 'Desirable' behavioural competencies for success in the role?

Key experiences required
• Identify which are 'Essential' and which are 'Desirable'

Knowledge required
• Identify what is 'Essential' and what is 'Desirable'

Qualifications and education required
• Identify which are 'Essential' and which are 'Desirable'

Key relationships
• Who are the key people that the role interfaces with?

Key performance indicators
• How do you know the role is being done effectively?

Recruiting into the team

If a role becomes available for replacement in an existing team structure, consider whether it really needs to be replaced. Similarly, if you think you need a new role adding to the team, challenge whether it is really required. Could work be reallocated between other roles? Does a role need to have a like-for-like replacement? Are there future changes you are aware of that will impact on the accountabilities and focus of the role? Don't automatically go out to recruit for the same role that existed previously.

The starting point for any recruitment process is to have a clear role profile in place. This ensures you know what you are looking for, and that people know what they are applying for. You want enough good quality, relevant candidates to apply, but not too many to deal with. As well as attracting applicants, the role profile should help potential applicants self-select out. It should be clear to them if they are not suitably qualified or experienced for the role. So you will need to produce a role profile, or review and update the existing profile.

When you've defined the role, or roles, that you want to fill, you must generate a pool of suitable candidates. You need to source applicants who meet, or can be cost effectively trained and developed to meet, the role requirements.

How you deal with applicants and potential applicants significantly impacts the view and perception of your business. This is true regardless of whether someone is ultimately successful with their application or not. Candidates are very likely to tell their friends and family about their experience, how they were treated and whether they felt their experience was a good or bad one.

You have a number of options for how to run your recruitment process. These could include

- managing the process yourself,
- asking a member of your team to run it,
- using your in-house team (this could be an HR, recruitment or administration team),
- outsourcing to an external HR consultant or specialist recruitment consultant,
- engaging a recruitment agency, or
- using a headhunter.

The option you choose will depend on a number of aspects. These factors include

- the type of role,
- the level of the role,
- the number of roles you are recruiting,
- the number of applicants you are expecting,
- whether the role is a scarce or specialist skill,
- how quickly you need to fill the position,
- the time you personally have available to manage the recruitment process,
- your level of skill in recruitment and selection,
- the budget available for the process, and
- whether the role is permanent or temporary.

Once you have your pool of applicants you then need to select the successful candidate. You must make sure that you use rigorous, fair, legal, robust and consistent selection tools and processes.

The format and style of the selection approach chosen will again depend on a number of factors such as company culture, the level and type of role, your industry or sector culture, the number of applicants, and the stage in the process.

It's key to remember that recruitment and selection is a two-way process. Whether a potential candidate wants to work with you is as important as whether you want to employ the candidate.

Below is a list of potential assessment and selection methods. Some will be more appropriate for your specific situation than others.

- Interviews
- Presentation followed by questions and answers
- Case studies
- Work simulations
- Portfolios
- Team tasks
- Tests for cultural or values fit - these may need to be run by a qualified person
- Ability tests - these may need to be run by a qualified person
- Personality or psychometric tests - these may need to be run by a qualified person
- Assessment centre – this approach combines several elements from the above list of options

Interviews are the most frequently used selection method so it's worth considering some of the potential format and style options in more detail.

The format of an interview is likely to be based on one of the following, or potentially a mix of these formats.

- Competency-based – focuses on past examples that demonstrate capability in the area of competence being assessed
- Situational – more theoretical and future focused
- Strengths-based – focuses on what a candidate is good at and the skills they enjoy using
- Technical and functional – focuses on the technical or functional skills and knowledge aspects of the role rather than behavioural aspects
- Unstructured – not good practice as it is less effective, not consistent and potentially unfair

The style of an interview is likely to be from one or more of these possibilities.

- Telephone
- Video conference – e.g. Skype, Zoom
- Face-to-face
- Individual (one-to-one)
- Group with a discussion topic
- Panel with two or more interviewers
- Formal
- Informal – for example over lunch or dinner
- Sequential – a series of interviews with different people

Regardless of the format and style of interview approach you choose to use, you must prepare suitable questions and use them consistently between candidates. These questions should produce evidence of the candidate's capabilities against the key competencies defined in the role profile.

It's also vital that you have a predefined scoring or rating method which is applied in a consistent way to all parts of the selection process. This will help to ensure fairness between candidates. The rating method should have some simple guidance for each level on the scale for the objective evidence you would expect to see against each competency.

When designing a selection process, consider the competencies that really need to be there at the outset and those that could be developed. It may be that you want to select a candidate with the attitude and values that fit with the team and then train some of the skill elements. However, it must be cost effective to do this and not have too much of a detrimental effect on initial performance.

You should define a threshold for each competency, below which a candidate would not be acceptable. Don't simply create a total score across all competencies. A candidate could score highly on all aspects except one. That one competency might be critical.

After an interview, or other selection method, rate the evidence gathered for each competency or aspect using the defined guidance so that you reach a score or rating.

To help reach a selection decision, put together a matrix which compares all candidates against each of the competencies required for success in the role.

Keep records and notes from the recruitment process for a reasonable length of time (e.g. three months). Good practice is to offer feedback to unsuccessful candidates, so having notes makes this process easier. There may also be a chance that an unsuccessful candidate challenges your selection decision. It will help if you have kept notes from the process. Destroy the notes after the defined time period.

It's essential to ensure that the people involved in the recruitment and selection activity are trained and competent to run a fair process. They must treat all candidates in a consistent and equal way.

How you deal with unsuccessful candidates is as important as how you treat successful candidates. Applicants who aren't successful will have a perception of the people they had contact with, and therefore the team or the business. Whether you agree or disagree with their perception is irrelevant. They will share their views with others and this could significantly impact the reputation of a business. Make sure you treat all applicants with the same level of care and dignity.

Once you've selected the successful candidate, note any gaps in their capability that will need to be filled when they join you. Build these aspects into their induction process or their initial training plan.

My Plans, Reflections, Ideas, Next steps and Thoughts

Skills and capabilities

---

*"Identifying individual skills and utilising them is
important to building a successful team."*
Amanda Strong, Mercia Image Print

It's important to have a detailed understanding of the
skills and capabilities of all team members. This will
ensure that the team as a whole has the range of skills
needed to meet its challenges and is capable to deliver
its purpose. Having a clear shared understanding at an
individual level allows the team to play to the members'
strengths and take advantage of them. Building on
strengths can increase the overall team performance
much more effectively than trying to develop individual
weaknesses.

Areas of skills and capabilities to consider can include

- Technical skills,
- Functional skills,
- Qualifications,
- Behavioural skills,
- Experiences, and
- Leadership skills.

When you've developed an understanding of the range
of team skills and capabilities, you can use that
information to identify gaps. These gaps could be filled
by recruiting to change the composition of the team
(bring in new people with new skills) or by developing

existing members. Decisions can also be made to change the mix of the team if it isn't optimised for what it has to deliver.

Depending on the nature and purpose of the team, it may be that the range, type and level of skills required changes over time. You need to review this regularly as the team makes progress against its challenges and deliverables through its lifecycle.

Use the process below to build an understanding of what the required skills and capabilities across the team are. Then assess the team members against them.

Step 1.

Take the team's purpose, challenge, deliverables and vision. Capture the range of skills and capabilities needed within the team to deliver them. Include information from the role profiles defined in the team structure work to supplement the list.

Aim to get full coverage of what's needed. What skills does the team as a whole need to succeed? Include technical, functional and behavioural skills, but also identify skills that are beyond the role profiles.

Identify the skills and capabilities needed.

Step 2.

Identify the key skills and capabilities that the team members already have. Make sure to include skills you know they have but don't use in their current situation.

Consider each member in turn and list their strengths.

Step 3.

Produce a matrix of how the skills and capabilities of the team members map to those needed.

An example skills and capabilities matrix is shown in Figure 4.

Skill or capability required	Member 1	Member 2	Member 3	Member 4
Financial analysis	x	x	√	x
Project management	√	x	x	√
Presenting	√	x	√	x
Negotiation	x	√	x	√
Human Resources	x	√	x	x
Team leadership	x	√	x	x
Etc				

Figure 4. Matrix of team member skills and capabilities against those required

Step 4.

Review the skills and capabilities matrix.

Ensure that there is a balanced spread of skills across all team members. Make sure that the team doesn't rely too much on one person to bring too many skills and capabilities to the team.

Step 5.

Identify where there are any gaps in skills and capabilities across the team or where the team is too reliant on one member.

What does the team need to be better at? Which skills could be developed by existing team members? Does the team need to recruit for any skills and capabilities?

What are the team gaps and development and recruitment needs?

Once produced, the skills and capabilities matrix should be kept up to date. The matrix can then be used for a number of different purposes.

- To identify training and development needs at an individual level. This could form part of an appraisal (performance management) and development review process.
- To feed into Individual Development Plans (IDPs) for team members.
- To produce team training plans which then form the basis of the training budget.
- To induct new members into the team.
- To share an understanding across the team of the range of skills and capabilities team members have available beyond their day-to-day role.

When you've got a detailed understanding of the team, its direction and training needs, you can start to work on individual team member development plans.

Using the information you've captured in the skills and capabilities matrix, you can now focus on what team members *really* want to, and need to, develop. There will be some gaps in team member skills, knowledge and behaviours, but you may not need to fill all those gaps.

If you build and improve on the strengths of the team members by a relatively small amount, then that could give you a far better return than trying to develop their weaknesses. Developing weaknesses could take a significant amount of time and cost. You may only move the weaknesses up to an 'OK' level with a substantial effort. Developing existing individual strengths may make the team exceptional in some areas. An individual's motivation to do something about their development is also likely to be higher if they are working on areas they're already good at and enjoy.

It's vital that you use the skills and capabilities matrix information to think through the areas which are worth development investment and those which are not. You can then start to build Individual Development Plans (IDPs) for each team member.

Step 1.

Look back at the skills matrix and identify the areas that individual team members *really* need to develop in order to achieve the team goals and deliver its vision.

What do individuals need to learn or develop? If you have a long list, assign a priority order.

Step 2.

Now you've identified what a team member needs, or wants, to develop you can think about how they'll develop. What solutions will you put in place?

Good development practice works on a 70:20:10 principle. This means that 70% of development should be from on-the-job experiences that are built into daily work tasks. This is most effective if there's a consequence of not improving in the area you're looking to develop. It also helps with motivation to develop. About 20% of development should come from approaches such as feedback, coaching, mentoring and observing others who are strong in the area you want to develop. The final 10% of development should come from courses, workshops and reading. Ideally you should combine a number of different solutions from each of the approaches areas to give maximum success.

What possible solutions could meet the development needs?

Step 3.

Once you've identified the development solutions, start to identify the resources and support needed to deliver the solutions. Resources could include time, money, support or advice. This activity will help you to make sure that the solutions you identify are viable. It will also help you to plan when, and how, to deliver them.

Capture the resources you need to deliver the solutions that you identified in Step 2.

What resources and support are needed?

Step 4.

Having identified the development needs, solutions and the resources required, it's important to define how you'll know when the development has been successfully achieved before moving on to developing another area. Success criteria could be achieving qualifications, receiving positive feedback around changes in behaviour, successfully delivering a project, reading a specific book and so on.

Capture the success criteria for the solutions you identified in Step 2.

What are the success criteria for each activity?

Step 5.

Set some timescales to complete the identified development solutions within. This will give focus and allow a plan to be produced to manage time, resources and activities effectively.

For each of the solutions you identified in step 2, and thinking about the resources and support needs from step 3, capture the timescales in which the development activity will be completed.

When will each of the development activities be completed?

Step 6.

Some individuals on the team may be members of a professional institute that has Continuing Professional Development (CPD) as part of its requirements. You can use the approach outlined previously to form part of a CPD plan and record. You then simply need to add a review of the learning and how it will be applied and used going forwards to complete a CPD record.

However, it's also good practice to carry out a review after the completion of any development activity even if there's no CPD requirement to do so.

Capture thoughts on the development activity that has been completed.

What has been learnt and how will it be applied?

My Plans, Reflections, Ideas, Next steps and Thoughts

Styles and preferences

"Ensure there is a diversity of skills, attributes and approaches to work. Teams are made up of individuals who should each be able to contribute in their own way."
Diz Lamb, Ardagh Group

Teams are made up of people, and each of those people is an individual with their own personality, preferences and style of working. There's no good or bad, right or wrong style or preference – just difference.

Members of exceptional teams need to value each other and value their differences and diversity. They can then maximise their own, and each other's, talents. It's important that team members know their colleague's strengths and compensate for their weaknesses so they can work together successfully.

A team member needs to have clarity of their own preferences and style, and how that affects the people they interact with. They can then positively impact and influence other team members. This also helps with the development of an understanding of others.

Once team members understand themselves, and their impact on others, they can start to adapt their behaviours and approaches. They will then work more effectively with their colleagues for the benefit of the team as a whole.

There are many tools and tests which can be used to help team members get more knowledge and understanding of themselves. Personality and occupational questionnaires explore aspects such as preferences and attitudes, motivations, interests and values, how people do things and how they are likely to behave in certain situations.

Using a consistent tool or test across the whole team can help to create a common language and shared understanding between team members.

Many of these psychometric tests need to be administered, and the results fed back, by trained and qualified test users. This ensures the best possible outcomes and value from the test and that the results can be explored and understood in detail through discussion. This will achieve the maximum benefit for the time and money invested.

Some examples of individual and team profiling tools and tests which can help team members understand their preferred ways of working are

- Myers Briggs Type Indicator® (MBTI)
- Sixteen Personality Factor Questionnaire® (16PF)
- Team Management Systems® (TMS)
- DiSC®
- Belbin® Team Roles
- Learning Styles questionnaire
- Insights Discovery®
- NEO Personality Inventory
- Occupational Personality Questionnaire (OPQ32)

It's important to get qualified advice and guidance about which tools and tests would be most appropriate to your team's particular circumstances and needs. It's also important to be aware of copyright if choosing to use tools and tests which don't require a qualification to administer, but should still be paid for.

In addition to taking a psychometric test or using a tool to understand your own, or team members' preferred ways of working, you could consider the following example questions and also add your own.

Think them through individually, or seek input from people you trust such as your partner or spouse, your peers, your boss, your team members, etc.

- How would I/you describe my style of working?
- How do I manage my time? Am I very structured or flexible?
- How comfortable am I with change?
- How do I prefer to communicate?
- Do I like time to think things through before I discuss my thoughts and ideas with others?
- What's my preferred working environment?
- How do I like to learn? Do I prefer to read about things first or try them out in practice?
- How do I make decisions? Do I make them based on logical analysis, or on my personal values?
- Do I enjoy being creative and generating ideas?
- Do I like to see things work in practice?
- How do I like to be rewarded?
- Is being recognised for my work important to me?
- Do I need to be around other people to be productive?

- How patient am I?
- What's my leadership style?
- How comfortable am I with delegation?
- Do I enjoy planning?
- Do I conform to rules and follow process?
- How comfortable am I with getting into detail?
- Do I enjoy meeting new people?
- How comfortable am I sharing personal information?
- Am I serious or lively?
- Am I a perfectionist?
- Do I avoid conflict or am I dominant?
- Am I trusting or suspicious of other people?
- Am I self-confident or do I doubt my ability?

Once you have some insights into your preferences and style of working, consider the following questions.

What are the key aspects of my preferences and style of working?

What's the impact of my preferences and style on the team?

What are each team members' preferred styles of working?

How do they differ from mine and from each other?

How can I adapt my style to help the other team members?

How can I help the team members adapt their styles to help each other?

How can our team exploit our differences?

My Plans, Reflections, Ideas, Next steps and Thoughts

Standards and behaviours

"A successful team always looks out for each other. Members should be team players and not just in it for themselves."
Mark Averill, 'AVIT! Media

Defining and agreeing a set of clear standards and behaviours for team member interactions may sound somewhat over the top. However, having a set of 'groundrules' can make a real difference to how a team performs. Defining these expectations removes any ambiguity and gives the team a framework of guidelines to work within.

A set of standards and behaviours also helps to build on, and support, the areas of commitment and alignment to the team, and its values. How team members behave is the visible representation and demonstration of their values. These behaviours then create the team culture. The culture of a team is "how things are done around here". Capturing and communicating the expectations around standards and behaviours can help new members to integrate into the team more quickly and effectively as they know what's expected of them from the outset.

Working with team members to develop their own set of standards and behaviours for the team will encourage their ownership, engagement and buy-in.

The expectations around standards and behaviours could cover areas such as

- Respect – for other team members and for the team processes
- Participation and involvement
- Contribution
- Collaboration
- Keeping promises
- Levels of trust

Consider these questions as a team to define the team's set of standards and behaviours.

What are our expectations of team member behaviour?

What are our team's Groundrules?

How should we enforce our standards?

How will we ensure that new team members buy in to our standards and behavioural expectations?

Teams comprising of members who behave in an unselfish way are more effective as a whole. This better and more effective team environment in turn creates better individuals who are motivated and want to be part of that team. The result is more stable team membership which generates a greater consistency of performance and results.

People – A personal example

Early in my HR career I was a member of an HR functional team. We met once a week to update each other on the projects we were working on, and to discuss ideas and strategies.

There was a colleague on the team at the same level as me and we just never hit it off. We were constantly butting up against each other and winding each other up in meetings. It wasn't a positive or helpful working environment for either of us.

A few weeks after I joined, the HR manager had a team away session and the whole team went through a Myers Briggs psychometric profiling activity. Myers Briggs looks at four areas of preference and I knew nothing about it at the time.

It turned out that the team member I didn't get on with and I were exactly the opposite on all four areas of the profile. He was an extrovert style and got his energy from talking and thinking things through out loud. I was an introvert style and got my energy from thinking things through first before talking about it. He was very detailed focused but I preferred the big picture. I was very logic driven and he was more values driven. He was very structured with his time whereas I was more energised by the last minute rush and comfortable with change. So we were very, very different.

However, we now realised it. We understood our differences and the reasons behind our conflict. It was simply different preferences and styles. There was no right or wrong style. From that point on we started to play to each other's strengths and preferences.

I now understood why he had to talk for the sake of it in the meetings (as I saw it). He understood why I sat back in the meetings and wasn't appearing to contribute at the time (as he saw it). If there was a task that needed some detailed activity doing he would work on it. If there was something that needed a bigger picture, more creative view, I would work on it. He would work on the programme management activity. I would carry out the logical analysis and he would consider the impact of the decisions on the people affected.

Therefore, we achieved a fundamental understanding of why we hadn't got on previously. Once we understood the reasons for our conflict we actually got on really well. We started to adapt our own behaviour so that we could help each other be more effective.

I started to progress up the organisation a bit faster than he did, and I actually became his mentor. So that understanding of our own, and each other's, styles and preferences fundamentally changed our relationship in that HR team. That change had a positive benefit to each of us at both a personal level and also at a team and business performance level.

People - Key learning points

- Teams are made up of individuals, and each of those individuals has their own drivers and motivations.
- Develop an in depth understanding of who the team members are at a personal level.

Structure and roles

- How the team is structured defines how the work is carried out and divided up between team members.
- Start with a blank sheet to structure a new team.
- Regularly review the structure of an established team.
- Consider the pros and cons of potential team structure options based on the team's challenges and deliverables.
- Consider the supervisory roles needed, depending on the number of team members. Aim to minimise the number of layers in the structure.
- Detail the responsibilities of each role within the structure and look for overlaps between roles to avoid duplication and confusion.
- Identify the skills, knowledge, behaviours and experiences required to perform each role successfully and produce clear role profiles.
- How you treat successful and unsuccessful applicants impacts the view and perception of your business.
- Use rigorous, fair, legal, robust and consistent selection approaches, tools and processes.

- Select an appropriate recruitment style and format that fits with your business culture and the role being recruited.
- Keep records and notes for a reasonable length of time and then destroy them.
- Offer feedback to unsuccessful candidates.
- Ensure those involved in the recruitment process are trained and competent to run a fair process.

Skills and capabilities

- Build a detailed understanding of the skills and capabilities of all team members.
- Ensure the team as a whole has the range of skills needed to meet its challenges and is capable to deliver its purpose.
- Building on existing strengths can increase the overall team performance much more effectively than trying to develop individual weaknesses.
- Produce a matrix of how the skills and capabilities of the team members map to those needed.
- Identify the team gaps and the development and recruitment needs.
- Produce team level and individual team member development plans.
- Use the 70:20:10 principle to identify development solutions.
- Identify the resources and support needed to deliver the solutions, the success criteria and the timescales.
- Review what has been learnt and how it will be applied.

Styles and preferences

- Value team members' diversity of style and preference. There is no good or bad, right or wrong style – just difference.
- Team members need to have clarity of their own style and preferences, and how that affects the people they interact with.
- Once team members understand themselves, and their impact on others, they can adapt their behaviours and approaches so that they work more effectively with their colleagues.
- Using a consistent profiling tool or test across the whole team helps to create a common language and shared understanding between team members.
- Seek qualified advice and guidance about which tools and tests are most appropriate to your team's particular circumstances and needs.

Standards and behaviours

- Standards and behaviours create the team's culture.
- Defining expectations removes ambiguity and gives the team a framework of guidelines to work within.
- Work with team members to develop their own set of standards and behaviours. This will encourage their ownership, engagement and buy-in.
- Use the team's standards and behaviours guidelines to integrate new members into the team.

My Plans, Reflections, Ideas, Next steps and Thoughts

Processes

"Spend time thinking about the team's processes and spotting areas for improvement."
Graham Schuhmacher, ex-Rolls-Royce

How the team operates from a practical perspective is another element for building an exceptional team. Understanding the processes that the team uses will help to get the work done effectively and efficiently. Defining and agreeing the team's basic, routine, and what could appear to be mundane day-to-day ways of working will bring benefits in performance.

As the team carries out its activities and makes progress, learning and knowledge should be captured and shared. This will help to avoid similar mistakes. It will also help other teams that may be picking up the work or doing similar projects or activities in the future.

The team will identify improvements as it performs its tasks. It may also be expected to identify and drive change. Improvements and change should be managed in a controlled way to avoid unnecessary business risk.

Defining structured ways of providing support in the form of feedback, coaching and mentoring to the team members is also key. This helps to develop members at an individual level, which ultimately benefits the team's capability, performance and productivity.

Ways of working

"There must be good communication within and between teams. Effective communication includes listening, so managing meetings so that contributions are heard and considered helps to build effective teams and processes."
Paul Naylor, Direct Help & Advice

For a team to operate effectively and efficiently there must be some standard ways of working, which members adhere to. This not only helps the established team members to work together, but it also helps with the induction and integration of new members into the team.

Spend some time thinking about the basic activities and processes that the team carries out on a day-to-day basis. For maximum engagement, the team members themselves should define the processes that they will work to.

For example, how will the team work in these key areas?

Meetings – a huge amount of time, and therefore money, is spent and wasted in meetings. These may be one-to-one discussions or involve larger groups. What regular meetings are really necessary? What's their purpose and frequency? Who should attend? How are they structured? How are actions captured and shared?

Communication – must be clear, unambiguous, open and timely between team members. How will they be involved and communicate with each other? What information and communication is needed and when? How will the team involve members who work remotely?

Problem-solving - create a safe environment where discussion, contribution, challenge, constructive criticism and analysis is encouraged. How will the team generate ideas and options to solve problems? How will they analyse and assess the options?

Decision-making – after the potential options have been analysed and assessed, decisions on the way forward need to be taken. How will the team make decisions? What decisions are the team empowered to make without referring to the leadership? What are the team's limits and boundaries? What's the team's approach to achieving consensus? Is there an ultimate decision maker?

Resolving conflicts – disagreement should be seen as positive and constructive in order to help create ideas, challenge and make improvements. However, there may be times when the team needs to resolve conflicts. How should conflicts be resolved in an open and transparent way? How should positive relationships be maintained when conflicts occur?

Integrating new team members – new employees, or existing employees who are changing roles and joining the team, need a structured, consistent and comprehensive induction process. How should new team members be inducted into an established team?

Spend some time thinking about each of these basic activities and processes. If possible, work through the questions as a team to generate ideas and to get team member agreement and engagement.

Meetings management

What regular meetings do we really need?

What's the purpose of each meeting?

What's the length of each meeting?

Who needs to attend each meeting?

Who should chair each meeting?

How should each meeting be structured? What should the agenda be?

How are actions captured and shared?

Who will capture and issue the action notes for each meeting?

What are the groundrules for how we run our meetings?

Here are a few tips for running effective meetings.

- Arrive 5 minutes early
- Be prepared – complete any pre-reading
- If you can't attend, send a properly briefed representative
- Start and end on time
- Put your phones and laptops away
- Have an agenda, send it out in advance, follow it
- Stay on the topic
- Listen generously – no interrupting
- Make your points briefly and concisely
- Share any relevant information and data
- Don't hold side conversations
- Disagree in a constructive way
- Silence means agreement, or make your point
- Everyone participates
- Send out action notes within 24 hours
- Complete your actions in the required timescales

Communication

What information needs to be communicated between team members?

When does the information need to be communicated?

What should the style and format of each communication be?

How will all team members be involved and communicate with each other?

How do we ensure all communication is clear, unambiguous and open?

How will we involve team members who work remotely?

Problem-solving

How will we generate options to solve problems?

How will we analyse and assess the options?

How will we create a safe environment where discussion, contribution, challenge and constructive criticism and analysis is encouraged?

Decision-making

What decisions are the team empowered to make?

What processes and approaches will the team use to make decisions?

What is the team's approach to achieving consensus?

What are the team's limits and boundaries?

Who is the ultimate decision maker if the team can't reach consensus?

Resolving conflict

How will we resolve conflicts in an open, transparent and positive way?

How will we maintain constructive relationships when we have conflict?

Integrating new team members

When bringing new members into the team, think about the experience that they will have. Start their induction process before they join the team. Once they have accepted a position, allocate a buddy to the new team member and make contact with them. Create a positive impression and build anticipation so they feel engaged with the team even before they officially join. Ensure that they receive the same quality of experience whether moving to a new role within the business or from an external organisation.

Once the new team member joins, have a phased approach to the induction information they receive. Don't try to do too much too soon. Have a plan for the information they really need to know on day one, and then what they need to know during their first week, their first month and maybe their first three months.

Structure the induction by considering these areas.

What are the health and safety aspects that new team members need to know?

What are the environmental aspects that new team members need to know?

What general administration and housekeeping aspects do new team members need to know?

What are the team cultural aspects that the new team member needs to know? Include content from the areas covered in this book.

What role specific aspects does the new team member need to know?

What immediate training needs does the new team member have? Include aspects arising from the selection process.

My Plans, Reflections, Ideas, Next steps and Thoughts

Learning and knowledge

"Mistakes are OK, but repeating the same mistake does not create a congenial atmosphere."
Jon Eno, Hot House Music Schools

As the team carries out its activities and makes progress, it's important that learning and knowledge is captured and shared. A structured approach to knowledge management helps team members to share the best practice that they develop. It helps to share the lessons that the team have learnt, to build on their achievements and avoid making similar mistakes within the team. It also retains learning and knowledge within the team when members leave.

Capturing learning and knowledge can help other teams across the business that may be picking up the work, or doing similar projects and activities in the future.

Storytelling is a particularly effective way of sharing knowledge and passing on experience. People enjoy listening to stories and tend to remember more of the content than from a standard presentation style. Help team members to capture and tell their stories.

A formal process and system for capturing and sharing knowledge, lessons, best practice and stories should be defined. However, the success of the knowledge management process depends on members recognising and understanding the benefits, and having the discipline to use it. They should be given time to capture their inputs or other priorities will take over. Work through these questions to build the team's learning and knowledge management process.

How will the team capture and record their knowledge and experience?

How will the team build the lessons learned into the processes the they use?

How will the team capture and share its stories?

How will the team communicate and share knowledge and experience with all of its members?

How will the team communicate and share knowledge and experiences with other teams in the business?

How will team members be given time to capture and share their learning and knowledge?

My Plans, Reflections, Ideas, Next steps and Thoughts

Improvements

---

*"Trust your team to make mistakes and learn from them.
This will make them better in the future."*
Sean Clare, Blue Arrow Derby

An exceptional team should continuously look to make improvements. These may be small steps or they could be significant changes. It's likely that the team will naturally find and develop improvements as it carries out its tasks. There may be an expectation placed on the team that part of its challenge is to identify, drive and experience changes and improvements. However, improvements and change must be managed in a structured and controlled way to avoid unnecessary business risk.

A culture in which new ideas are welcomed, discussed, constructively criticised and analysed needs to be developed. Innovation and creativity should be encouraged, and mistakes seen as OK – as long as they are learned from. The status quo should be challenged appropriately, but not simply for the sake of it. Challenge and change should result in benefits to the way the team works, the delivery of the project and its outcomes, and ultimately to the wider business.

Team members should also consider the areas they individually and collectively need to be better at. They should use those thoughts to identify their development needs and build them into their development plans.

The Exceptional Team Blueprint™

Work through these questions to develop how the team will identify and manage improvement ideas.

How will we encourage innovation, creativity and new ideas?

What processes will we put in place to capture and analyse improvement suggestions?

What improvement tools and techniques will the team deploy?

Should we reward team members for making improvements? If so, how?

What does the team need to be better at?

What are the team's specific development needs and how do these feed into individual development plans?

My Plans, Reflections, Ideas, Next steps and Thoughts

Support

"Provide 1-to-1 coaching of individuals to ensure they understand their role purpose and how it fits with others in the team. Provide feedback on performance and seek input on how the leader can improve their support."
Graham Schuhmacher, ex-Rolls-Royce

Defining and implementing formal support processes for team members is vital to learning and performance improvement. Having structured ways of providing feedback, coaching and mentoring is key to developing an exceptional team. This helps to develop members at an individual level, which ultimately benefits the team's capability, performance and productivity.

Feedback

Clear, consistent, timely and on-going feedback will help all team members improve at a personal level and at a professional level. Create a safe environment, built on trust, in which team members can give and receive feedback and share and exchange views and ideas with each other. Ensure feedback given is relevant, fact-based and focused on improvement. Encourage individuals to be a 'critical friend' to their colleagues.

Just as importantly, help team members to be open and receptive to feedback from their colleagues. Encourage them to review and consider the feedback and act on it.

Work through these questions to develop a process and culture for giving and receiving feedback in the team.

How can we create a safe environment in which team members can give and receive feedback?

How do we encourage team members to be a 'critical friend' to their colleagues?

How do we ensure that clear, relevant, consistent, fact-based and timely feedback, focused on improvement is given on an ongoing basis?

How do we help team members to be open to receiving feedback from their colleagues?

> How do we help team members to act on feedback?

Mentoring

A mentor is an experienced person who provides high-level, long-term developmental and growth support to a less experienced person (the 'mentee'). They give help, guidance and advice and are usually skilled in the field of work in which the mentee wants to progress. Mentor support is typically related to career progression activities and professional growth, and is an on-going relationship. Mentors don't generally observe and advise on specific actions or behavioural changes in daily work activities.

Mentors are usually more senior and experienced employees from the mentee's business. This means they are familiar with the organisational culture and politics that the mentee is working within.

A mentoring relationship can bring benefits to both the mentee and the mentor.

Some benefits for the mentee are

- Access to someone with an interest in their field of work
- Broadens perspective and knowledge
- Offers insights into formal and informal company structures
- Helps build self-confidence
- Brings heightened self-awareness through constructive feedback
- Supports career planning and networking
- Provides a sounding board for ideas
- Brings a different perspective to careers advice
- Helps meet the development requirements of professional institutions

Some benefits for the mentor are

- Contributes to personal and professional development
- Improves awareness of the perspectives of less senior staff
- May prompt a reassessment of their own ideas and approaches
- Develops and provides practice in a range of skills
- Identifying of future potential leaders
- Enhances peer recognition
- Increases job satisfaction
- Offers an opportunity to extend their personal network

Mentors and mentees should be aware of their specific roles and responsibilities in how the relationship will operate. A 'contracting' activity should be carried out at the start of the interaction to clarify what the mentor can and can't, and will and won't do for the mentee.

How do we encourage team members to work with a mentor?

How do we identify the aspects a mentor is needed to help with?

How do we identify and engage appropriate mentors?

Coaching

A coach can be engaged to help correct individual (the 'coachee'), or team, behaviours that detract from their performance. They can also help to strengthen behaviours that support improved performance around a set of activities to achieve a specific goal. A coaching relationship is typically a shorter term, finite duration focusing on immediate impact and improvement.

Coaches can work at an individual and team level. They encourage team members to think through challenges and develop their own options and solutions. This is achieved using a structured framework approach based on questioning techniques to create new thinking.

The Exceptional Team Blueprint™

Coaches are often brought in from outside the business to address a specific issue. However, it can be very effective to train team leaders and team members in coaching skills so that they have the capability to coach each other on a day-to-day basis.

A coaching intervention can bring benefits to both the coachee and the coach. The coach particularly benefits if they are an internal employee of the business.

Some benefits for the coachee are

- Provides access to independent support
- Improves current individual performance
- Improves ability to find solutions to solve specific issues
- Develops self-awareness
- Improves a specific skill or behaviour
- Corrects performance or behavioural difficulties
- Enhances ownership and responsibility
- Increases motivation
- Increases job satisfaction

Some benefits to the coach are

- Enhances engagement and involvement
- Increases satisfaction
- Develops and provides practice in a range of skills
- Improves managerial and leadership capability
- Enhances respect and trust
- Increases talent retention
- Improves individual and team performance

Coaches and coachees should be aware of their specific roles and responsibilities. A 'contracting' activity should be carried out at the start of the interaction to clarify what the coach can and can't, and will and won't do.

Coaching interventions are generally more structured than mentoring relationships. The most widely known coaching framework is the 'GROW' model. However, there are a number of other frameworks such as 'ITGROWS', 'FUEL', 'CLEAR' and 'CEDAR'.

How do we encourage team members to work with a coach?

How do we identify the aspects a coach is needed to help with?

How do we identify and engage appropriate coaches?

Would the team benefit from team coaching as well as individual coaching?

Do we want our team members and leaders to develop coaching skills so they can coach each other?

Processes – A personal example

Whilst at Rolls-Royce I was asked to join a project team that was established to develop a bid submission for a £7bn civil nuclear decommissioning contract. The team was a joint venture and consisted of members from Rolls-Royce, AMEC and Atkins.

The team was led by an exceptional Project Director. When I joined it was impossible to tell who was from which parent organisation. I asked him how he selected the team members. He replied that he took the technical or functional capability of the candidates as a given. He assumed that the parent companies would only put forward capable people. He therefore selected based on how the potential members would fit into the team culture he wanted. His approach worked.

The nature of the project meant that we were working very long hours and many of us were away from our home and family all week. We effectively worked, lived and socialised as a team 18 hours a day. This created a very strong team spirit and supportive culture.

There were 24 workstreams across the project and I led one of them. It was critical that all the workstream teams knew what the others were doing and how their work impacted on each other. Because of the fast pace of the project, and a constantly shifting customer specification, we needed to have very structured processes and ways of working. Particular emphasis was placed on communication, meetings management, decision-making and knowledge and information sharing.

A project room was set up which was the hub for these aspects. The room was kept locked when not in use due to the sensitivity of the project. Within the room, each workstream had a section of wall to display our current strategies, plans and solutions. Project team members could go into the room to look at the latest status and thinking of the workstreams that affected them. This encouraged and ensured the capture and sharing of knowledge, information and learning.

Communication sessions were held daily at 9am in the project room. During these 30 minute meetings, the Project Director shared any changes and key decisions that had occurred during the previous 24 hours. Workstream leaders then shared any highlights and key changes from their areas that may impact others in the team. On a Monday morning, the communication session lasted an hour and went into more detail about the plan and key deliverables for the coming week.

A structured programme of regular weekly and monthly meetings was set. These meetings focused on reviewing progress and making decisions. Only relevant team members attended, there were specific agendas set, and preparation and completion of actions was expected.

Open and honest feedback was given on the content and quality of the strategic papers that were written. Support from peers or senior leaders was always available to any team members who were struggling with any professional or personal issues.

From a total perspective, this was the best experience of team working I had during my corporate career.

Processes - Key learning points

- Understanding the processes that the team uses will help to get the work done effectively and efficiently.
- Defining and agreeing the team's basic, routine ways of working will bring benefits in performance.

Ways of working

- Spend time thinking about the basic activities that the team carries out on a day-to-day basis.
- Define the processes the team will follow for these activities
  - Managing meetings
  - Communication
  - Problem-solving
  - Decision-making
  - Resolving conflict
  - Integrating new team members

Learning and knowledge

- Define a process and system for capturing and sharing knowledge, lessons learnt and best practice.
- The success of a knowledge management process depends on team members recognising and understanding the benefits, and having the discipline to use it.
- Give team members time to capture their learning and knowledge.

- Storytelling is an effective way of sharing knowledge and passing on experience. Help team members to capture and tell their stories.

Improvements

- Develop a culture in which new ideas are welcomed, discussed, constructively criticised and analysed.
- Innovation and creativity should be encouraged, and mistakes seen as OK as long as they are learnt from.
- Improvements and change must be managed in a controlled way to avoid unnecessary business risk.

Support

- Create a safe environment in which team members can give and receive feedback and share and exchange views and ideas with each other.
- Ensure feedback is relevant, fact-based, clear, timely and focused on improvement.
- Help team members to be open and receptive to feedback. Encourage them to act on it.
- A mentor is an experienced person from within the business who provides high-level, long-term developmental support to a less experienced person.
- Mentor support is related to career progression and professional growth and is an on-going relationship.
- A coach helps correct behaviours that detract from performance or supports activities to achieve a goal.
- A coaching intervention is a shorter term, finite duration focused on fast impact and improvement.

My Plans, Reflections, Ideas, Next steps and Thoughts

Performance

"Continually focus on the goals and the people. It's a bit like driving a car. You need constant observation and small adjustments to make sure that everyone is happy and everything is on track."
Diz Lamb, Ardagh Group

In order to ensure that your team is making the most efficient and effective use of its time and other resources, it's important to know how things are going. How is your team performing against its challenges and what it has to deliver? Is it making the progress you'd expect? Do the team members know how they're performing? Who else needs to know about the team's progress and performance?

The team needs to have a set of goals and objectives that are defined to support their deliverables at both a team and an individual level. These goals and objectives need to be built into a structured plan which identifies the resources needed to achieve and deliver them.

The stakeholders who have an interest in what the team is doing and the progress it's making need to be identified. The measures of team performance should then be specified so that only useful data is generated. Finally, the reporting requirements for the team should be understood so that the data collected is translated into useful information for the stakeholders.

Goals

"An effective team is one which knows exactly what their goals are, so that key steps towards achieving these are followed and processes developed."
Paul Naylor, Direct Help & Advice

The team needs to break the achievement of its vision, strategy, challenges and deliverables down into a number of goals. These goals should be used to build a plan which will help the team achieve each one and, ultimately, deliver its strategy, meet its challenges and move towards its vision.

Break the high level vision, challenges and deliverables down into smaller chunks and set the team goals around them. Make sure the goals you define are clear and demanding, but also binary (so you can tell whether they've been achieved or not), specific and unambiguous. Identify goals that will stretch the team members, without being too daunting. Stretch goals can provide an additional level of motivation and drive to achieve them.

Ideally involve the team members in setting the goals. If the team members aren't involved in their definition, make sure the goals are shared with the team and that the team members understand them and engage with them.

Set a number of goals which can be used to form a plan covering a reasonable period of time. For example, you could set one year goals, six month goals, three month goals and one month goals. These can then be used to build a weekly activities list if needed.

The team doesn't need to work on all its goals at once. It's probably better if it doesn't as that could result in overload. Focus on a few goals, achieve them, and then move on to the next ones. Review the goals regularly and set further ones as you need to.

You may be familiar with the well-known method to use when setting your goals – the 'SMART' approach.

Your goals should be

- S – specific and strategic
- M – measurable and meaningful
- A - achievable and action-oriented
- R – realistic and results-focused
- T - time-bounded and tangible

There are some views that this SMART approach to objective and goal-setting limits your thinking. My view is that you can set goals at different levels. The team's big goal (its vision) can be as stretching, challenging and audacious as you like. However, your shorter term goals and objectives, which form the steps that help you achieve your big goal, need to follow the SMART approach. These goals will form the practical approach that you'll take to develop your plan.

The team level goals can be used to form the basis of the performance management process for the team members – whatever form that process takes. Goals should be converted into objectives at an individual level. Each member must be clear on what they have to achieve and how they contribute to the team's vision.

What is our team ultimately here to deliver? Refer to the work in the 'Purpose' section.

What are the key 'chunks' of work that need to be delivered to achieve the team's vision or meet its challenge?

How do the chunks of work fit together from a timing perspective?

One year

6 months

3 months

1 month

Define 'SMART' team goals based on the chunks of work identified.

My Plans, Reflections, Ideas, Next steps and Thoughts

Planning

"Communicating plans for the business, plans for progression and any particular project they're on is key. Most frustration comes from people who feel 'left out in the dark' not knowing which direction they are headed."
Rob Twells, Frogspark

The team now needs to start to take some actions to achieve its goals and move towards delivering its vision. This can be done by building the defined goals into a plan. You can either use the goals as they are, or break them down into smaller steps, activities and tasks to help with your planning.

Start with a longer term plan, say a twelve-month plan, with some higher level goals and then break that plan down into a greater level of detail. Develop plans of goals and activities for six months, three months and one month but make sure that the plans build up and support each other.

If appropriate, use the monthly plan to define weekly and daily team tasks. This will help the team manage its time more effectively and efficiently.

Use simple project management tools and techniques to build the plan and to define the main tasks that will help with the delivery of each of the team's goals.

- Prioritise the goals and tasks into a timeline of the order that they need to be completed.
- Look for tasks that depend on the completion of other activities first, and use that information to set the sequence.
- Estimate the time needed to complete each task.
- Make sure each task and goal has a specified date by which it must be completed.
- Consider and identify the resources that will be needed to perform and complete each task successfully. Resources could include people, money, time, tools and equipment, skills or specific behaviours.
- Identify the resources that are available and those which are missing and you need to find.
- Allocate an owner to each task who will be responsible for its delivery.

Define the team's plan by considering the following.

What are the main goals or tasks we have to achieve?

What tasks are dependent on the completion of other activities first?

In what order do the goals and tasks need to be completed?

What date does each goal and task have to be completed by? Create a timeline.

What resources will be needed to perform and complete each task successfully?

What resources are available and which are missing?

How will we obtain the missing resources we need?

Allocate an owner to each task who is responsible for its delivery.

My Plans, Reflections, Ideas, Next steps and Thoughts

Measuring

"Only use the minimum, simple to understand KPIs to run the business activity."
Graham Schuhmacher, ex-Rolls-Royce

In order to measure the team's progress and performance you'll need to define a set of Key Performance Indicators (KPIs). Base the KPIs on the team's challenge, its deliverables and the goals that have been set. But don't have too many.

Make sure the KPIs are relevant, clear and have measurable criteria, supported by data that can be gathered easily. Monitor the team's performance against the KPIs on a regular basis as it works on the tasks and towards achieving its goals and deliverables.

Decide what you'll do if the team isn't on course and the KPIs start to indicate that it may not deliver the goals. Consider how the team will correct their performance and progress so that things are put back on track and the goals are delivered.

Ensure the KPIs are visible to the team members so they can see how things are progressing. They can then take action to proactively address any issues that are arising.

Define a set of Key Performance Indicators (KPIs) by considering these questions.

What KPIs should our team be measuring so we know we are making progress?

How do the KPIs link to our team challenge and what it has to deliver?

What data will need to be collected to report the KPIs?

Who will capture the data?

How often will we capture the data?

What will the team do if the KPIs show it's off course and may not deliver its goals? How will the team correct its performance?

Where and how will we display our KPIs so they are visible to the team?

My Plans, Reflections, Ideas, Next steps and Thoughts

Reporting

"Regularly brief the team on performance against mission KPIs. Highlight areas hitting targets and areas needing to improve. Use the team to highlight issues stopping them succeeding."
Graham Schuhmacher, ex-Rolls-Royce

Developing an understanding of who the team's stakeholders are will avoid wasting time and effort producing information and sending out reports that no one reads.

A stakeholder is someone who has an interest in how the team is performing and the progress it's making. Stakeholders could be internal or external to your business. Depending on the type of team you lead or are part of, some examples of stakeholders are customers, suppliers, bosses, team members, peers in other functions, parents, students, trustees, funders or government agencies.

Work through the questions to ensure you only provide and report relevant information that your stakeholders want, in a format they want, and when they want it.

It's likely that different stakeholders will have different requirements. You must understand their specific needs. This will ultimately save your team's time by only reporting information that's wanted, will be looked at, and acted upon.

Who are the team's key internal stakeholders? (People within the business).

Who are the team's key external stakeholders? (People outside the business).

What information do the stakeholders want to know about how the team is progressing and performing? This may vary so consider and ask each stakeholder.

Internal stakeholders

External stakeholders

How does the information required link to the Key Performance Indicators (KPIs) identified earlier? If it doesn't, review the KPIs.

How often do they want to receive the information and update? Consider and ask each stakeholder.

Internal stakeholders

External stakeholders

What format do the stakeholders want the update in?
How do they want to receive the information?
Consider and ask each stakeholder.

Internal stakeholders

External stakeholders

Performance – A personal example

One of my corporate roles was the Head of Early Career Pipeline. My team covered education outreach activities and the recruitment, selection and development of apprentices and graduates for the global business. I had 50 people working for me and we were responsible for approximately 2,000 trainees in the business. We managed over 14,000 applications a year and recruited around 1,000 young people on an annual basis.

When I moved into the role I was given some time to review the current state of the Early Career Pipeline team. I had to develop a proposed strategy and way forward, whilst running the day to day activities. I broke the activity down and created a plan of each goal and task that my team and I had to deliver.

I began by looking at the overall purpose of the team and the various sub teams. I spoke to each of my team members individually and formed my first impressions of the strengths and challenges within the team.

There was some fantastic work being done already by the team. However, one of the main concerns I had was the significant amount of time taken, and disruption caused, by ad hoc requests from the team's stakeholders for data and reports. These requests distracted the team from their main responsibilities.

There was a significant number of stakeholders that the team had to manage. These included the team members themselves, the trainees currently in the business, managers looking after the trainees on attachments, suppliers of agency staff and education providers, skill owners, senior managers, successful and unsuccessful applicants, the trainees' parents, professional institutions, OFSTED, government departments, schools, universities, the internal HR and Finance functions. The list went on.

I reviewed the existing structure and proposed the formation of an Early Career Business Management team. This team would become responsible for the definition of the KPIs that would be used to measure the performance of the Early Career team. They would produce a standard monthly performance pack and dashboard that addressed the most frequently asked questions and data requests. They would produce monthly financial and highlights reports. They would develop and administer a trainee database to track where the trainees were on attachment within the organisation.

This approach was designed to minimise the number of one-off requests for specific data and reports. Of course there would always be some, particularly from senior managers to answer external questions. However, the vast majority were addressed and eliminated.

The proposed change to manage, measure and report data and team performance more effectively was well received by my seniors and by the team. It allowed team members to focus on the areas of work they were originally employed to do, that they were most effective at, and that they enjoyed. It also allowed the specific recruitment of people who were skilled in, and enjoyed, dealing with data.

Performance - Key learning points

- In order to ensure that your team is making the most efficient and effective use of its time and other resources, it's important to know how things are going from a progress and performance perspective.

Goals

- Break the high level vision, challenges and deliverables down into smaller chunks and set the team goals around them.
- Identify goals that will stretch the team members, without being too daunting. This provides motivation and drive to achieve them.
- Set a number of goals which form a plan covering a reasonable period of time.
- Your shorter term goals should be
    - S – specific and strategic
    - M – measurable and meaningful
    - A - achievable and action-oriented
    - R – realistic and results-focused
    - T - time-bounded and tangible
- Involve the team members in setting the goals so they understand them and engage with them.
- Use team level goals for the basis of the performance management process for the individual team members.

Planning

- Start with a longer term plan with higher level goals and break that plan down to a greater level of detail.
- Use project management tools and techniques to define the main tasks required to build the plan.
    - Prioritise the tasks into a timeline of the order in which they need to be completed.
    - Identify tasks that depend on the completion of other activities to set the sequence.
    - Estimate the time needed to complete each task.
    - Define a specific completion date for each task.
    - Consider and identify the resources needed to perform and complete each task successfully.
    - Identify the resources that are available and those which are missing and you need to find.
    - Allocate an owner to each task who is responsible for its delivery.

Measuring

- Define a set of Key Performance Indicators (KPIs) to measure the team's performance and progress.
- Make the KPIs relevant and clear, with measurable criteria supported by easily gathered data.
- Monitor performance against the KPIs regularly.
- Decide what you'll do if the KPIs start to indicate the team may not deliver the goals.
- Make the KPIs visible to the team so they can see their progress and take any necessary action.

Reporting

- An understanding of the team's stakeholders will avoid wasting time and effort producing information and issuing reports that no one reads.
- A stakeholder is someone who has an interest in how the team is performing and the progress it's making.
- Provide and report relevant information that your stakeholders want, in a format they want, and when they want it.
- Stakeholders will have differing requirements. Understand each of their specific needs.

My Plans, Reflections, Ideas, Next steps and Thoughts

Team leadership

> *"Work hard to demonstrate that you have your people's best interests at heart. You will gain their trust and they will give much more than you give them."*
> **Simon Bucknell, EMBS**

I've been extremely fortunate to work for several great leaders during my career. Each of them brought and demonstrated different strengths in their leadership style that made them successful in my view. I've identified and captured some of those key strengths, observations and lessons from my experience of a number of them. Some of the aspects link directly to elements of the Exceptional Team Blueprint, whilst others are more behavioural.

You don't need to be in a formal leadership position to improve the performance of the teams you're a member of. You can think about and use many, if not all, of these aspects to help your fellow team members be part of an exceptional team.

Create vision and direction

Create a compelling vision of what your team has to deliver. Ensure the team members understand the reasons why they are working to achieve that vision. This sets and communicates a clear direction for the team.

Inspire

Sell the vision to your team and inspire them to want to achieve it. Help the team members identify what's in it for them as they move towards the vision. Define the personal benefits that will result for them by achieving the vision.

Set stretch goals

Create interest, challenge and motivation by setting goals that will stretch your team and move its members out of their comfort zones. But don't stretch them too far as that can cause stress. Do this for goals at both a team and an individual level.

Focus on 'what' not 'how'

Generate ownership and engagement by clearly defining what you want your team members to deliver. Then let them work out how to achieve it and the tasks they need to do in order to make it happen. Don't tell people how to do it, but be available to advise and provide as much support as they need.

Build two-way trust

Build trust with your team members by doing what you say you will do and meeting any commitments you make to them. Don't micro-manage the team, but trust the team members to get on with what they need to do in order to deliver the tasks and goals.

Involve and engage

Involve all your team members by seeking and valuing their input and ideas. Listen more than you speak. Engage them in the bigger picture and encourage them to participate.

Identify and remove obstacles

Help your team to deliver and achieve by identifying obstacles. Listen to concerns about the barriers and the problems raised by the team. Help them to remove the obstacles completely, or minimise the impact that they have. Encourage the team to define their own solutions.

Resolve conflict quickly and directly

Deal with conflicts between team members and those with people outside the team in a timely way. Be direct and clear on the way forward to resolve the issues.

Be supportive

Accept that mistakes will happen. Support team members who make mistakes whilst they work to deliver tasks. Ensure they learn from the things that don't work first time and that they share their learning across the team.

Participate

Be prepared to be an active member of the team when needed. Be willing to get your hands dirty to help the team move towards the vision.

The Exceptional Team Blueprint™

Show appreciation

Give genuine, timely and frequent appreciation and recognition to individual team members. This could be for aspects such as delivering tasks, generating ideas, putting in significant discretionary effort, supporting other team members at an emotional level, or demonstrating the team behaviours in a positive way. Make sure the appreciation is in a form that the team member wants and values.

Recognise when team members step out of their comfort zone to fulfill requirements. They should be praised for their determination and willingness to take risks.

Spot potential in individuals

Think beyond the immediate team and business needs and identify potential for growth in individual team members. Work with them and help them to develop so that they can achieve their potential. One of the key roles of a leader is to identify and develop their successors.

Understand and care about individuals

Build an understanding of the members of your team and how they like to work at an individual level. Consider how your preferences and style impacts on others. Adapt your style to make things easier for someone who likes to work in a different way to you.

Be decisive

Make a decision, even if it's the wrong one. People get more frustrated by a lack of decision-making than by a leader making the wrong decision.

Be humble

Respect other's views. Be honest and admit when you're wrong and be willing to say sorry. Give credit to others when it's due. Put others first, before yourself.

Give time

Be available and approachable for your team members when they need you. Be ready to listen.

Demonstrate the team values

Team members will look to you to demonstrate the values in everything you do. They will model your behaviour. Think about the 'shadow of the leader'. The 'shadow' you cast through your behaviour reflects what you see as important. Recruit team members who align to the team's values and live the values yourself.

Be authentic

Be true to yourself and don't pretend or try to be someone you're not. Behave with integrity. People will see through it if you're trying to portray an image that isn't you.

Give honest feedback

Be transparent about the performance of the business, the team and individuals. Give both positive and developmental feedback. Be open, timely and honest with feedback and address problems as they arise.

Continue to develop

Invest in your own development so that you continue to grow at both a personal and professional level. Also invest in the development of your team members.

Communicate

Effective communication underpins much of these leadership aspects. Communicate effectively and check that you have been heard and understood. Ensure you listen in return.

Be confident and positive

Be confident and believe in who you are and what you are doing otherwise nobody else will. Remain positive and upbeat. Bad things will happen but you always have a choice as to how you react.

Be willing to share leadership

Recognise that team leadership may shift in order to drive and deliver results. Sometimes the formal team leader may not necessarily be the best person to lead on a certain aspect or task. Encourage team members to take a leadership role when appropriate.

Work hard, play hard and have fun

Create a team environment that encourages and rewards effort and hard work, but also ensure that team members enjoy what they do. Generate an atmosphere in which team members enjoy each other's company at a social level as well as a business level.

Team leadership – A personal example

One particular team leader stands out to me from my corporate career. When I asked for his input as part of my research and validation for the Exceptional Team Blueprint, these were his responses.

To the question "What do you think are the three most important aspects of building a successful team?"
1. Take time to choose the right people: people with the right skills, behaviours and attitude. Mistakes are costly.
2. Delegate meaningful work and give people responsibility and accountability for delivery.
3. Bring the team together (socially/physically if possible), talk business, recognise contributions and achievements - and have some fun.

To the question "What are your top three tips for being a great leader?"
1. Give praise and recognition in public as well as privately.
2. Give time to team members. Be available and approachable and always be pleased to see team members.
3. Be humble, be the occasional butt of a joke, smile.

He got to know his team on a personal level as well as a professional level. He had very high expectations of engagement, performance and commitment. He held team away events. These events mixed business aspects with social and relationship building activities in memorable ways that really pulled the team together.

Team leadership - Key learning points

- Create vision and direction.
- Inspire.
- Set stretch goals.
- Focus on 'what' not 'how'.
- Build two-way trust.
- Involve and engage.
- Identify and remove obstacles.
- Resolve conflict quickly and directly.
- Be supportive.
- Participate.
- Show appreciation.
- Spot potential in individuals.
- Understand and care about individuals.
- Be decisive.
- Be humble.
- Give time.
- Demonstrate the team values.
- Be authentic.
- Give honest feedback.
- Continue to develop.
- Communicate.
- Be confident and positive.
- Be willing to share leadership.
- Work hard, play hard and have fun.

My Plans, Reflections, Ideas, Next steps and Thoughts

Team environment

> *"Cultural alignment is important. In an existing team, recruit to fit the existing culture and values. In a new team, align to the work but identify what culture do we really want?"*
> **James Blake, Talk Staff Group**

Two key aspects contribute to creating the environment in which the team operates.

1. The 'culture' that the team creates, i.e. the cultural environment.
2. 'Where' the team works from, i.e. the physical environment.

Cultural environment

Culture is often defined simply as 'how we do things around here'. It is therefore driven and determined by the behaviours of the team members and leaders.

The cultural environment of a team will be influenced by working through the sixteen areas of the Exceptional Team Blueprint and embedding them in the team's day-to-day activities. However, there are a number of broader areas which are described below that impact on the cultural environment of the team.

Creating a shared team identity in which members think "we" first rather than "I" is a great foundation for an exceptional team. This builds the attitude and culture that the members succeed or fail as a team, not as individuals.

A supportive atmosphere should be developed. All team members must feel confident and able to speak up and be heard without fear of rejection or embarrassment. This will encourage input, ideas, ownership and engagement from team members and therefore positively impact on team performance.

The team should be focused on hitting goals and given the autonomy to do what's needed to deliver. Members should be empowered to work within defined decision boundaries and limits and trusted to deliver.

Team members should care about each other and care about each other's growth and success. Ideally the team should socialise together sometimes, as well as work together. However, it's important that this isn't forced on people.

Ultimately, any team exists to deliver a result for the business or the organisation. The team atmosphere should be positive and success-focused. Achievements and successes should be recognised and celebrated as a team. Consideration could also be given to some form of team-based reward, but this will depend on the environment and culture in the wider business.

A culture should be created in which team members genuinely enjoy working in the team and with each other. If they have some fun whilst they're doing it then that can create some real enthusiasm and energy.

Physical environment

The physical environment in which the team operates must support and enhance the cultural environment you want to create within the team. This is particularly important where the team is co-located.

Whilst there will usually be some practical and budgetary constraints, involve the team members as much as possible in creating and developing their physical working environment.

The physical environment needs are likely to vary depending on whether the team is working on a project with a defined end date or whether it is a permanent work team. Each team situation will be different and will drive different needs.

An open plan layout aids communication, sharing of information, ideas generation, and helps to build relationships. However, this can be distracting for some team members depending on their style and preferred ways of working. Provide breakout areas where members can go to work in a quieter space or to make phone calls. Set up meeting spaces which are separated to stop noise transfer. Offer private rooms in which to have confidential calls and discussions.

Providing different desk arrangements can also help members with different working styles. For example, you could include unallocated desk groupings (hot desks), standing desks and more informal areas to generate the opportunity for conversations.

If a team is working on a specific project, it can be very effective to provide a separate lockable team room. This may also be necessary from a confidentiality and security perspective.

In addition to offering private meeting space, this allows project team members to display information about the area of the project they are working on. They can display material such as their strategies, ideas, plan and progress. Other team members can see the latest status of aspects that may have an impact on their area of responsibility. This information can be permanently displayed so it is easily accessible to all team members, but must be kept up to date.

If there is no dedicated team room, it's still important to have information boards around the team's workspace. These should be used to display the Key Performance Indicators that have been defined to measure and report the team's performance and progress. Again, this information must be kept up to date.

Team environment – A personal example

In my role as Head of Early Career Pipeline I was responsible for the global processes for developing young people in a FTSE100 engineering business.

This started with delivering education outreach activities in schools to encourage pupils to study maths and science and consider a career in engineering. The process moved through work experience and intern placements and into the attraction, recruitment and selection of apprentice and graduate trainees. It was completed by the management of the apprentice and graduate training schemes and the output of capable people into the business.

The desired team culture was one of openness, with one joined up team looking after the end-to-end early career processes. There was a large co-located team based in Derby and a number of small teams based in global locations including America, Norway, Germany and Singapore.

The Derby-based team was structured around the key high level processes of education outreach, attraction and recruitment, apprentice development and graduate development. The team sat in an open plan office. There was no allocated seating and a small amount of personal storage was provided in portable under desk units and a fixed locker. A larger storeroom was available for shared resources. The intention was to enhance communication and information sharing within the sub-teams and across the full team.

The nature of the work of the team meant that trainees frequently came into the office to ask questions. The office therefore needed to be a welcoming and approachable environment. Separate small rooms were provided throughout the building for confidential conversations and calls. A larger meeting room at the end of the office was used for team and customer meetings.

There were informal meeting and discussion areas positioned around the building in which the office was located. Team members often held information sharing discussions in a café area that was available for those based in the training centre.

This layout of the office and the availability of different spaces for conversations helped develop the one team and open culture in Derby. I held weekly management team briefing and communication meetings with my first line reports and monthly briefings for the whole team. I covered the remote teams using a combination of telephone and video conferences and met face-to-face when possible.

In order to aid information sharing and progress reporting, an Early Career Pipeline Performance Pack was developed. This was used to share information and performance against the Key Performance Indicators across the team members and also with stakeholders outside the team.

A very positive and committed team atmosphere was created, with all team members focused on delivering the best possible experience to the team's customers.

Team environment - Key learning points

- Two aspects contribute to creating the environment in which the team operates.
  - o The cultural environment.
  - o The physical environment.

Cultural environment

- Determined by the behaviours of the team members and leaders.
- Work through the sixteen Exceptional Team Blueprint areas to help create the team culture.
- Create a shared team identity.
- Develop a supportive atmosphere.
- Trust and empower members to hit the team goals.
- Encourage team members to care about each other.
- Generate a positive, success-focused atmosphere.

Physical environment

- Must support the desired cultural environment.
- Involve team members in creating the physical environment.
- Consider different working style preferences when designing the layout.
- Create opportunities for communication.
- Consider the need for a lockable team room.
- Ensure team performance data is visible.

My Plans, Reflections, Ideas, Next steps and Thoughts

Remote teams

"Many teams are no longer co-located and a lot of time and effort can be wasted with insufficient or ineffective communication. Those teams who utilise technology and are imaginative about how they communicate and create a sense of team belonging tend to do best."
Diz Lamb, Ardagh Group

It's becoming increasingly likely that team members won't all be co-located. Depending on the size and nature of the business and the work being carried out, members may be based at a mixture of a 'head office' location, in remote offices elsewhere in the country, at their home, or in overseas locations.

The move to virtual and global working presents particular challenges to building an exceptional team. Team members working remotely should be treated and managed in the same way as in-house or local team members as much as is practically possible. This will make them feel they are part of the team instead of a hired resource. In turn, this will drive them to work harder and be more committed to the team and its vision, goals and deliverables.

This chapter discusses some of the main areas that need to be considered when working with remote team members.

Relationship building

Strong relationships are critical to building exceptional teams. But how do you create relationships between team members who work remotely? If possible, team members and leaders should meet face-to-face at least once to build the initial relationship.

However, it may not always be practical to meet physically so video conferencing technology such as Skype or Zoom should be considered. Try to use video conferencing in the same way that you would if you were meeting face-to-face. Give people time to speak in turn, allow them to introduce themselves, ask them questions and listen to their answers.

Getting to know remote employees on a personal level helps to build rapport with the team. Team leaders should take time for casual conversations and small talk with their team members, instead of just discussing a project's requirements. If they're prepared to, encourage team members to share information about things outside the working environment as well as work-related aspects. However, be aware of cultural differences in terms of how much personal information people are initially willing to share.

Encourage team members to continue to use video conference facilities where possible. This will help to keep building relationships more effectively than phone calls where they can't see each other.

Team members could show warmth towards their colleagues who work remotely by sending gifts such as company merchandise. These will make the remote workers feel more engaged and connected to the team and the business, thereby strengthening the relationships.

Setting the foundations

When people are working remotely from the main team location, it's essential that they are very clear on the team's vision, values, challenges, deliverables and desired team culture.

Wherever possible, the remote team members should be involved in the creation of the vision and the definition of the values. If they can't be physically present when the vision and values are produced, they should be shared with them and their views sought before being finalised. The remote team members will then feel more ownership and engagement with the vision and values.

The challenges, deliverables, goals and requirements of the team should be clearly described to the remote team members. Any queries regarding the team's project or activities should be answered fully to avoid confusion and ensure they are fully understood.

Involve the team members who work remotely in the definition of the expectations around the standards and behaviours which define the team's culture. Remote team members will bring a different perspective about how they contribute. They may have issues and problems which are unique to their situation. If it's not possible to involve them in the definition, then communicate the expectations to them and seek their input, feedback and agreement.

Communication

Effective on-going communication with remote team members will positively influence the productivity of the team and its activities. Technology offers a common workspace for team members where they can connect, collaborate, share and find the information regarding the work to be done.

Tools and technologies (such as Skype, Zoom, WhatsApp, FaceTime, Google Hangouts, Dropbox, SharePoint) have made communication much easier. These provide opportunities to enhance the interactions between the local and remote team members and leaders. They also help the team by allowing the leaders to clearly convey the expectations and goals to the remote members. A key consideration when sharing information and sending documents should be security.

Working with globally-based team members may mean that it's important to take the language barrier into consideration. If English is the business language, but isn't the first language of a team member, don't talk too quickly and avoid using jargon and colloquialisms.

If you're employing outsourced team members who are working remotely, it may be worth starting with a small pilot project with them. This can be used to work out any communication issues before starting the main project or activity.

Meetings

Meetings involving remote team members should be well planned. Online meetings via methods such as Skype, Zoom or Google Hangouts should be scheduled to discuss the team's progress and to work through any problems faced by team members. Identify overlapping working hours of team members and arrange meetings at a time when as many members as possible will be available.

Use the checklist below to plan meetings and make them effective and efficient.

- What regular meetings do we really need?
- What's the purpose of each meeting?
- What's the frequency of each meeting?
- What's the length of each meeting?
- Who really needs to attend each meeting?
- Who should chair each meeting?
- How should each meeting be structured?
- What should the agenda be?
- How are actions captured and shared?
- Who will capture and issue the action notes for each meeting?

A particular problem in meetings with remote attendees is that the people who are located together in a room for the meeting start to have side conversations between themselves. Participants who are linked in via video or audio conference call become excluded as they can't hear what is being discussed and they become disengaged.

It's also much easier for participants to be distracted when taking part in online meetings or conference calls. This is particularly true for audio conference calls when some members aren't visible to the other attendees. Therefore, clear groundrules for the online meetings should be set to ensure all attendees can contribute effectively.

Cultural awareness and sensitivities

Behaviours and ways of working that are culturally acceptable in one country may not be acceptable in another. Invest some time researching and understanding the business and personal cultural norms and etiquette for the countries of the team members you're working with. Beware of stereotyping however as there will always be variations between individual attitudes. Show respect to other cultures and use your understanding as general guidance until you get to know a team member well.

Some of the possible areas to be aware of include

- the amount of time it takes to create trust and build personal relationships
- the expected hierarchies and structure in an organisation
- the attitude to bosses and the recognition of the role of the leader
- business etiquette such as whether to shake hands, how to pass business cards and what to do when you receive one, meeting style when you meet face-to-face

- the concept of 'face' - how to disagree with someone without causing them to lose face
- expected dress code in business situations
- how to refer to someone - use of names and titles
- attitude to time and punctuality
- willingness to discuss and share personal circumstances and family situations
- attitude to rules and process compliance
- negotiation style and approach
- communication styles
- attitude to reward and recognition
- local public holidays and festivals

Time zone awareness

Managing time zone differences can be one of the biggest challenges when working across global regions. Identify whether there are any overlapping hours when both local and remote team members will be available. These hours should be used for real-time sharing of information about the work or project, discussing issues, progress updates, learning and feedback.

Be aware of time zones when arranging calls. Consider varying the start times of calls or meetings so that the remote team members aren't always the ones who are inconvenienced.

Manage team member, leader and stakeholder expectations around response times to emails. Don't expect an immediate response to emails that are sent during the local team members' working day to remote team members when it is outside their normal working hours.

Planning and monitoring work

As the leader of a team with remote members, it can be a challenge to plan, monitor and control the work of people who aren't co-located with you.

A starting point is to make sure that you have regular contact. Set up weekly communication calls, by video or phone, so that you both know there is a planned opportunity to speak. Make it clear that you are also available in between these planned calls if they need to contact you for any reason.

When you ask a remote team member to do a specific task, make sure they are totally clear on what they have to deliver. Check their understanding of the expectations placed on them and give them time to ask questions. Discuss their progress on the regular communication calls but don't micromanage them. Trust them to deliver.

In order to manage time and availability across the wider team, use a shared calendar. Keep track of regular meetings, local public holidays and team member time off. This will help to avoid last minute project interruptions due to team members being unexpectedly unavailable.

Set up a regular full team communication meeting (say on a monthly basis). Use this time to review team member tasks, responsibilities and progress. Allow members to raise issues and concerns at the meeting, but also encourage communication between local and remote team members between the planned meetings.

Remote teams – A personal example

One of my roles was as the HR Director for the Marine Services division at Rolls-Royce. I was based in Singapore but the members of my HR team were located globally. They were structured on a regional basis in the UK (also covering the Nordics), the USA (covering North and South America), The Netherlands (covering Europe and Africa) and Singapore (covering Asia and Oceania).

I tried to arrange to meet face-to-face as a full team at least once a year (subject to budgets) as it was important to build personal relationships. During these sessions we planned on a longer term, strategic basis and worked on building an understanding of each other's individual styles and preferences.

The team members had differing levels of experience and therefore required differing levels of support, coaching and mentoring. I held individual calls with each member once a week. On these calls we discussed their progress on the tasks they had to deliver and talked through any specific issues they were experiencing.

The time zone difference between Singapore and the USA made full team calls quite difficult, but I was fortunate that my team members were flexible with their time. We held regular monthly team conference calls to discuss issues and updates about what was happening in each region. This allowed the sharing of learning, knowledge and experience across the team.

Remote teams - Key learning points

- It's increasingly likely that team members won't all be co-located.
- The move to virtual and global working presents particular challenges to building an exceptional team.
- Aim to treat team members who work remotely in the same way as in-house or local team members.

Relationship building

- Try to meet face-to-face at least once.
- Use video conferencing technology.
- Take time for casual conversations and small talk.
- Encourage team members to share information about things outside the working environment as well as work-related aspects.

Setting the foundations

- Ensure that remote team members are very clear on the team's vision, values, challenges, deliverables and desired team culture.
- Involve remote team members in defining the expectations around the standards and behaviours.
- Seek their input, feedback, views and agreement if they can't be involved in creating them. This will build engagement.

Communication

- Use technology to facilitate effective communication with remote team members.
- Consider any language barriers. Avoid using jargon and colloquialisms and don't talk too quickly.
- Start with a small pilot project with remote team members to work out any communication issues.

Meetings

- Identify overlapping working hours of team members and arrange meetings at a time when as many members as possible will be available.
- Plan and structure meetings to make them effective and efficient.
- Define clear groundrules for online meetings to ensure all attendees can contribute effectively.

Cultural awareness and sensitivity

- Behaviours and ways of working that are acceptable in one country may not be acceptable in another.
- Research and understand the business and personal cultural norms and etiquette for the countries of the team members you're working with.
- Beware of stereotyping. There will be variations between individual attitudes.
- Show respect to other cultures.

Time zone awareness

- Identify any overlapping hours when local and remote team members will be available.
- Be aware of time zones when arranging calls.
- Manage expectations around the response times of remote team members.

Planning and monitoring work

- Plan regular contact with remote team members and be available in between these planned calls.
- Check the understanding of the expectations placed on remote team members, give them time to ask questions and check progress regularly.
- Use a shared calendar to manage time and availability across the team.
- Set up a regular virtual full team communication meeting. Review tasks, responsibilities and progress, raise issues and concerns.

My Plans, Reflections, Ideas, Next steps and Thoughts

Team Charter

"Your team is more important than anything else in your business – including revenue. A good, motivated team will bring revenue anyway."
David Torrington, Sky Recruitment Solutions

A Team Charter captures and summarises the areas of the Exceptional Team Blueprint in a single place. It provides a reference for team members to explain the focus and direction of the team and defines 'how things are done around here'. It is effectively the team's 'license to operate'.

The aspects covered in the Team Charter content should be those that the team members see as key. These will vary depending on the team's situation, its maturity and its life-cycle stage. Investing time to develop a Charter will help to clarify the team's objectives and approach. The Charter also provides the information needed to enable team members to get things right first time and reduces the risk of rework.

A Team Charter is most effective if it's created as the team is forming. However, existing teams will benefit from the process of defining a Charter at any stage. It's essential that the Charter is created together as a team. This generates shared understanding across the team and encourages ownership, engagement and buy-in.

As well as being a reference source for existing team members, a Charter helps with the induction of new team members. They can be taken through the Charter in a structured way over a period of time. This saves the new members having to find out how the team works through hearsay and trial and error.

Team Charter content

Content areas for the Team Charter could include;

- Purpose of the team
- Challenge and deliverables facing the team
- Team vision and values
- Commitment expectations of team members
- Team structure and role profiles
- Team member skills and capabilities
- Team member styles and preferences
- Standards and behavioural expectations
- Ways of working – the team processes
- Capturing and sharing learning and knowledge
- Identifying and implementing improvements
- Team member support approaches
- Team goals and objectives
- Planning methods used by the team
- Monitoring and measuring team progress
- Reporting team progress
- Who is the team's senior level sponsor?
- Team members and leader names and roles
- Key stakeholders of the team
- Duration – how long the team will be together?
- Support required - people and resources
- Key links outside the immediate team

Team Charter format

It's important that the Team Charter is simple, useful, easy to read and easy to access. Team members must want to use the Charter as a reference. Other recipients and stakeholders must see it as adding value to them.

The format chosen for the Team Charter will depend on a number of factors such as the team's situation, the resources available and the range of circumstances in which it will be used.

Potential options for the format could include

- an electronic version available to all team members on a shared drive
- a physical copy given to all team members
- a summary poster displayed in a team room and around the team's working areas. The poster could be signed by all team members to demonstrate their commitment to working to the Charter
- an electronic or physical copy given to the team's stakeholders

The actual content and level of detail given in each option may vary. This detail would depend on the purpose of the option chosen and the intended audience.

The Team Charter should be a living document that is reviewed regularly. It must be kept up to date and relevant with the team's latest thinking and processes.

Creating the Team Charter

The Team Charter should be created with the involvement of all team members. This will help to build team engagement and buy-in to the principles and content. The creation of the Charter could also be combined with an opportunity to build relationships within the team.

One option is to use a structured, facilitated workshop approach. This could be held away from the normal place of work in order to minimise the likelihood of interruptions and distractions. At least a day should be set aside to create the Charter. However, if team member relationship building is also a goal for the session, then a two-day event could be designed. Specific team building activities would then be scheduled into the event.

There may be a need for some follow up work to be carried out after the session. A final review meeting would be held before the Team Charter is complete and ready for issue.

If it's not practical to involve all team members in a workshop, an alternative option is that the leadership team produce a draft Team Charter. This draft is then taken to the team members for their review, feedback and input prior to final agreement and publication.

The key objective for the creation of the Team Charter, whatever approach is taken, is that all team members feel engagement and ownership. They must be committed to work to the principles defined in it.

Team Charter – A personal example

I was a member of a multi-disciplinary project implementation team tasked with the building of a new machining facility. I led the HR sub-team on the project working alongside colleagues who looked after other sub-teams such as technical, logistics, finance, building, IT and programme management.

We held a specific 'Team Day' at an offsite venue with the goal of creating the Team Charter. All the implementation team members and leaders attended. The workshop followed a structured approach and it was designed and run by a skilled facilitator from outside the team.

We began by agreeing the high level content areas that the Charter needed to cover. This was done as one large team.

The content list defined for the Charter was as follows.

- Implementation team 'pledge'
- Team purpose
- What are our individual team objectives and roles?
- What are our key tasks and processes at a sub-team level?
- What are our deliverables?
- Who are our customers and suppliers?
- How do we do our job?
- Implementation team structure and members
- Team groundrules

We were then split into our sub-team groups and we worked up the detail for our specific areas of responsibility.

A plenary session was held with the full team back together. During this session, each sub-team shared their detailed work. Other team members questioned and challenged (in a constructive way) in order to improve the Charter content. This also made sure it was easy to understand without specialist knowledge.

Finally, as a full team we defined our ways of working. These included meetings, communication methods, decision making, conflict resolution, processes, approval levels, documentation structures, and the team groundrules.

After we'd completed and agreed the content, every member of the implementation team signed the Charter. This demonstrated our buy in and commitment to work to it.

The Team Charter was printed into A6 sized booklets and a copy given to all team members and key stakeholders. A copy was also given to new team members as they joined and it was used as a key part of their induction into the team.

Finally, posters of the implementation team 'pledge' were produced and these were signed by all the team members. The posters were positioned around the team office and the new facility once it was occupied. This demonstrated the team's commitment to the new culture, team behaviours and environment.

The Exceptional Team Blueprint™

Team Charter - Key learning points

- A Team Charter provides a reference for team members to explain the focus and direction of the team and defines 'how things are done around here'.
- A Team Charter helps with the induction of new team members. They can be taken through it in a structured way over a period of time.

Team Charter content

- The content should capture and summarise the areas of the Exceptional Team Blueprint.
- The content should cover those aspects that team members see as key.
- The content and level of detail will vary depending on the team's situation, its maturity and its life-cycle stage.

Team Charter format

- The Team Charter must be simple, useful, easy to read and easy to access.
- The format will depend on the team's situation, the resources available and the range of circumstances in which it will be used.
- The format could be physical copies or electronic versions on shared drives.
- The Charter should be a living document that is regularly reviewed, kept up to date and relevant.

Creating the Team Charter

- The Charter should be created with the involvement of all team members to build engagement, buy-in, ownership and commitment.
- Use a structured, facilitated workshop approach to create the Charter.
- Specific team building activities could be built into the event.
- If all team members can't be involved, the leadership team should produce a draft Team Charter. This is then taken to the team members for their review, feedback and input prior to final agreement and publication.

My Plans, Reflections, Ideas, Next steps and Thoughts

Helping teams with change

"Change is constant, uncertainty is constant and the ability to steer through this and help others to deal with this now 'normal' environment is vital."
Diz Lamb, Ardagh Group

Some of the changes your team goes through will be viewed as positive and some will be viewed as negative. There may not be a choice about the change that is happening, but team members can choose how they react to the change and how they approach it.

In any change that you're involved with, don't expect to have the full picture and don't aim for perfection. If you do, you may never make the change happen. Identify and manage the risks as you go through your change, but tolerate mistakes and learn from them.

You could think about your change as a trapeze. If you hold on to the same bar, you'll keep swinging and will stay in the same place. But if you let go, and grab the next bar, it may be uncomfortable as you fly through the air, but you'll end up in a new place.

Use the following process to help your team to make the changes they're going through, or need to go through, more likely to be successful and comfortable.

Step 1.

Recognise the need or the driver for the change. Create the team's change vision and approach around it.

What's the need, driver or reason for the change?

What's the vision and approach to the change you are looking to make?

Step 2.

Build a network of support for the team made up of people you trust. Let them know what the change is that the team is working on and ask for their help.

Who could form the support network and how can they help the team succeed?

Step 3.

Allow the team members to set goals that take them outside their comfort zones and move them towards the change they need to make.

What are the team members' goals?

Step 4.

Get the team organised, take action on the first goal, and start to do things differently.

> What are the practical things that the team needs to get in place to start working on, and delivering, their goals for the change?

Step 5

If you feel that team members are resisting the change, understand the reasons why. Develop ideas to help them feel comfortable and able to move on.

Why are team members (or you) resisting the change?

What can you do to help overcome resistance?

Step 6

Celebrate successes as the team achieves each goal they set. Then move on to the next goal and achieve that one.

What can you do to celebrate success as the team achieves each goal?

Step 7.

Keep the team focused on the vision for the change.
Build and embed the new habits and behaviours.

What difference do people now see?

What are the benefits to the team members of having successfully achieved the change?

Helping teams with change – A personal example

I was working as a Head of Employee Development in Derby when one day I got a call from my boss. He said that the organisation was setting up a new division and asked me if I wanted to be part of the new executive team as the HR Director. I immediately said yes as I saw it as a great opportunity. He then told me that the role was based in Singapore. I said in that case I'd better talk it through with my family before accepting! It then became a change management task.

I'd only been to Singapore on a three-day conference before so I'd basically seen a hotel. Jo, my wife, had never been. We really would be going into the unknown. At the time, Jo was running a pre-school, Hannah and Emily (twins) were just starting senior school, and Tom was five. I talked it through with Jo and we agreed that it was a fantastic opportunity and experience for us all. It really was once in a lifetime, and if we said no then we'd regret it and wouldn't be asked again.

The next evening we gathered the children together and explained to them what we were being offered. As a selling point, we showed them pictures of Singapore and some of the surrounding countries that we could visit during our time there. Emily's response was "am I dreaming?" so we knew we had another of the team on board. We decided to go for it and I formally accepted the role the following day.

We then had to tell our parents and siblings. Although we were moving to the other side of the world, they were all incredibly supportive. That may have been partly due to the potential holiday opportunity, but it was important to us.

Jo and I went on a four day pre-visit to find somewhere to live and a school for the children. When we came back we had to start to plan the move and prepare to let our UK property so that we had somewhere to come back to at the end of the assignment.

The leaving parties were difficult, particularly Hannah and Emily's, but we were then on the way. When we landed it would be the first time the children had seen what would be their home for the next few years. Tom, whose legs didn't reach the end of the seat on the plane, stayed awake for the whole of the thirteen-hour flight and high fived the cabin crew as he left got off.

Keeping in touch was easy – almost too easy - through Skype and email. We had many visits from family and friends. Some several times.

It was a fabulous opportunity for us all. We experienced many new cultures, lived as minorities in another country, and visited some awesome places for our holidays. We took it in turns to choose where we wanted to visit. The children went to a school with only about 400 pupils, but 42 nationalities. They now have friends all over the world, and an incredible understanding of other peoples' views and situations.

The assignment was initially for two years but we ended up staying for over four. It was certainly a team change management activity that worked out well.

Helping teams with change - Key learning points

- You may not have a choice about the change that is happening, but you can choose how you react to the change and how you approach it.

A process to help teams with change

- Recognise the need or the driver for the change. Create the team's change vision and approach.
- Build a network of support made up of people you trust. Let them know what the change is and ask for their help.
- Allow the team members to set goals that take them outside their comfort zones and move them towards the change they need to make.
- Get the team organised, take action on the first goal, and start to do things differently.
- Understand why team members are resisting the change. Develop ideas to help them feel comfortable and able to move on.
- Celebrate successes as the team achieves each goal. Then move on to the next goal and achieve that one.
- Keep the team focused on the vision for the change so that they build and embed the new habits and behaviours.

My Plans, Reflections, Ideas, Next steps and Thoughts

Team member wellbeing

"Put others first before yourself. Put other peoples'
wellbeing before your own."
Mark Averill, 'AVIT! Media

The wellbeing of team members and leaders is now recognised as an essential focus for businesses and organisations.

By implementing a holistic approach to wellbeing – taking into account physical, mental and financial aspects - businesses can move towards becoming an employer of choice. Focusing on team member wellbeing can result in improvements in recruitment, retention, attendance, engagement and ultimately performance.

The cost of replacing a team member who leaves a business is often quoted as being an average of around £30,000. Clearly this depends on the salary level involved, but also takes into account agency or recruitment costs, management time, lost productivity, overtime for other employees to provide temporary cover, retraining costs and time, and reduced effectiveness whilst a new employee is learning the job. What's your level of employee turnover? What's the cost of replacing an employee in your team? If you can improve your employee retention level, then you could save a significant amount of money.

A survey by Global Corporate Challenge identified that 'presenteeism' costs businesses ten times more than absenteeism. Employees were reported to take an average of four days off sick per year. But they admitted that they are unproductive whilst at work for an average of 57 days a year. That's three working months.

There are now potentially five generations of employees in the workplace - Traditionalists, Baby Boomers, Generation X, Generation Y (or Millennials), and Generation Z. But is each of these different generations motivated by the same things from work? Do they all want to work in the same way? What's their attitude if they see their colleagues from a different generation wanting to work and be led in a different way to them?

Employees report that they want the following from an employer of choice. Many of these aspects link directly to wellbeing.

- A great place to work – a collaborative and open culture
- Flexibility in hours and time working on site
- Benefits that promote their lifestyles
- Workplaces that don't have to be in the office
- A high degree of autonomy
- Career growth, fulfilling work and stability
- Equality of treatment in their professional and personal lives
- A focus on what you do, not where you work from

There are said to be two types of stress. Productive stress helps to get things done, and is something we all need to drive us to perform to the best of our abilities.

The Exceptional Team Blueprint™

Unproductive stress is damaging to the individual and to the business. It can be caused by team members having to comply with unrelated and irrelevant rules that don't help get the job done. These rules add no value to the business. Unproductive stress is frequently caused by inflexible working constraints.

People work and perform better at different times. Some prefer to start earlier and finish earlier. Others prefer to start and finish later. When employees feel they have some control and autonomy over when, and how, they work they are less stressed. Work-life balance initiatives such as flexible scheduling choices are increasingly demanded by employees. These approaches allow employees to work undistracted by the family and life events and needs that are occurring outside of the workplace. Allowing some flexibility around working time can also help to improve the diversity of team members.

The New Economics Foundation (NEF) developed 'Five ways to wellbeing'.

1. Connect – with people around you. Build and focus on relationships at work and in your personal life.
2. Be active – take part in physical activities.
3. Take notice – be curious and be aware of things around you.
4. Keep learning – learn new things and accept challenges.
5. Give – do something positive for others, volunteer, and thank people.

Consider how these 'Five ways' apply to you, and how you could apply them to your team situations either as a team leader or as a team member.

Alternatively, Reed, the recruitment company suggest these tips to improve wellbeing.

- Boost team relationships – promote a fun and sociable atmosphere. Allow everyone a voice.
- Mindfulness – encourage meditation, effective breathing techniques and yoga. Switch off digital devices and take time out.
- Focus on posture – ensure team members carry out their jobs to the correct health and safety standards.
- Healthy choices – eating, drinking and exercise.
- Recognition – encourage and support individual's goals and aspirations using tailored incentives.
- Find problems – uncover underlying root causes through discussion and understanding.

Some businesses, particularly larger ones, put in place external support systems. These take the form of Employee Assistance Programmes (EAP) and helplines.

Managing stress

Some level of stress can be of benefit in the work environment. It can motivate and be a trigger for action. However, when stress becomes a regular occurrence and lasts for long periods of time, the effects on our physical and psychological wellbeing can be disastrous. Elevated stress levels can lead to many health problems and have a negative impact on our work and home life.

There are many ways we can reduce stress to ensure we're performing at our best and looking after ourselves. Below are a few simple thoughts which can start to help. A holistic approach to stress management is vital and elements such as sleep, exercise and positive activities mustn't be over looked.

Step 1. Take a break.

When we're feeling stressed, our bodies release cortisol and adrenaline. This in turn stops the functioning of the part of our brain we need to concentrate and focus. Taking a break allows you to relax and allows your brain to work to an optimal level. Breaks should be taken every couple of hours, must be enjoyable, and must give you the opportunity to switch off completely.

Write down some ways in which you can enjoy a break.

Step 2. Look at the questions you're asking yourself and rephrase them.

Our brain works to serve us in the simplest, most efficient way. The questions we ask ourselves are vital as we can only expect a direct answer. For example, if someone asks themselves "Why can I *never* meet a deadline?" the response they get will be equally negative, "Because you work too slowly."

Consider how rephrasing these questions could have a more positive response. "How can I meet a deadline?" may be met with "Prioritise your work load so that this is completed before anything else."

Make a list of some of the negative questions you ask yourself and then write the same questions but rephrased to bring a more positive response.

Step 3. Examine your work-life balance.

Most people get on with day-to-day life without taking the time to look and assess if they are truly happy, or where areas need improvement. When our work-life balance is healthy we generally feel less stressed. There's no right or wrong level of work-life balance. It will vary significantly between individuals. However, it's important to think about what level is best for you.

Write a timetable of a typical day and whether you find your usual activities enjoyable or unenjoyable. Look at ways the unenjoyable activities can be reduced or made more enjoyable. Examine the things that drain you and see if they really need doing every day. Assess the things that bring you joy. How can they be increased?

Step 4. Assess your diet and level of exercise.

In order to reduce stress, it's important to look at the food you're eating. It's generally thought that foods that increase our blood sugar levels have a negative impact on stress. A healthy level of B vitamins are said to have a positive impact on reducing stress.

Exercise is also vital to decrease stress and improve your health.

Write a food and exercise diary of a typical day for you. Where can you replace some foods with a healthier alternative? Where can you build in exercise?

Step 5. Keep organised.

A disorganised state can lead to stress. When you organise your day or your week, you know what's expected of you and can plan how to achieve it. Of course, things will occur which you'll have to react to.

Make a list of the activities and obligations you need to do on a daily or weekly basis. Allocate times for each of these. Allow some extra time for unexpected events.

Implementing wellbeing approaches

Team member and leader wellbeing is now a big focus for businesses. It's moved from being a 'Nice to do' to a 'Have to do'. Look outside your industry or sector to benchmark how other companies manage wellbeing. Create your unique selling points to differentiate your business from your competitors in the wellbeing area.

Implementing a holistic approach to wellbeing could require a significant cultural and mindset shift in your business. You may need to introduce wellbeing elements and initiatives in an incremental way, using small steps to make progress.

Consider how you measure team member performance. Focus on their outputs rather than inputs. Focus on the root causes of underperformance of team members rather than absence. Value team member productivity over presenteeism.

Ultimately, many of the initiatives and interventions around wellbeing require trust in order to succeed. That trust starts at the top with the leaders in the business, and the shadow they cast through the teams and the organisation.

Team members will look to the leaders to demonstrate trust in them. They will examine how seriously the leaders take wellbeing from a personal perspective. From that they will decide how seriously the business takes the wellbeing of their employees.

Team member wellbeing – A personal example

When I was Head of Early Career Pipeline I was responsible for a team that was much more diverse than most of the rest of the engineering business. To manage and encourage that diversity, my main focus was to develop a team culture with a flexible approach to working time and working location.

This required me to demonstrate a high degree of trust in my team members. We developed a set of team level goals and objectives that we had to deliver for the year. These were then broken down and cascaded to each team member to define their individual objectives.

Team members managed their own working time, and also the location from where they worked. If they needed to come into the office a bit later sometimes, or leave a bit earlier then that was acceptable. Similarly, if they needed to leave for a couple of hours during the day, or work from home, then that was OK as well. Sub-teams within the department developed their own local 'rules' to ensure there was always a team member present to deal with any face-to-face enquiries.

The fundamental understanding was that they delivered their objectives. I monitored their outputs and performance rather than their attendance in the office.

This culture of give and take resulted in the team members being highly committed. If they needed to work longer to ensure they delivered a task then they were motivated to do so.

The Exceptional Team Blueprint™

Team member wellbeing - Key learning points

- The wellbeing of team members and leaders is an essential focus for businesses.
- Deploy a holistic approach to wellbeing – consider physical, mental and financial aspects.
- Focusing on wellbeing results in improvements in recruitment, retention, attendance, engagement and performance.
- There are two types of stress
    1. Productive stress helps to get things done.
    2. Unproductive stress is damaging to the individual and to the business.
- Different generations in the workplace are motivated by different things. They want different ways of working and want to be led differently.
- People work and perform better at different times. If they feel they have control and autonomy over when and how they work they are less stressed.

'Five ways to wellbeing'

1. Connect.
2. Be active.
3. Take notice.
4. Keep learning.
5. Give.

Reed.co.uk tips to improve wellbeing

- Boost team relationships.
- Encourage mindfulness.
- Focus on posture.
- Healthy choices.
- Give recognition.
- Find problems.

Managing stress

- Take a break.
- Look at the questions you're asking yourself and rephrase them.
- Examine your work-life balance.
- Assess your diet and level of exercise.
- Keep organised.

Implementing wellbeing approaches

- Look outside your industry to identify best practice.
- Implementing a holistic wellbeing approach may require a cultural and mindset shift.
- Focus on team member outputs rather than inputs.
- Focus on underperformance rather than absence.
- Value productivity over presenteeism.
- Many wellbeing initiatives require trust to succeed.
- Trust starts at the top of the organisation.
- Team members will look to leaders to demonstrate trust in them.

My Plans, Reflections, Ideas, Next steps and Thoughts

Identifying priority development areas

"Don't waste your time, money and energy developing areas you don't need to. Prioritise what really needs to be developed to drive your team forward."
Andrew Deighton, AWD Development Solutions

Unless you're starting up a new team, it's extremely unlikely that you'll need to focus on developing all the areas of the Exceptional Team Blueprint at the same time. Your priorities will depend on the type of team, where the team is in its lifecycle, the experience level of the team members, any specific situations or issues, your budget and time you have available. However, it's essential to focus initially on the key areas that will make the biggest difference and have the largest impact on the team's performance. This will ensure that resources are used as effectively and efficiently as possible, and that you get the greatest return on your development investment.

In order to decide where to focus, use the prioritisation grid shown in Figure 5.

Firstly, consider how important each of the aspects from the Exceptional Team Blueprint is in terms of driving the performance of the team forwards. Work through each in turn and rate them 'High', 'Medium' or 'Low' importance. Make sure you think about the future importance of an aspect based on the direction of the team and not just its current importance.

The Exceptional Team Blueprint™

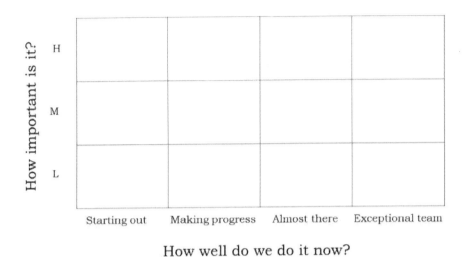

Figure 5. Prioritisation grid for identifying Exceptional Team Blueprint areas for development.

Next, consider the current capability of the team against each aspect. Work through each in turn and rate them 'Starting out', 'Making progress', 'Almost there' or 'Exceptional team'.

After rating each aspect against the two criteria, it will fall into a specific box on the prioritisation grid. Position all the Blueprint aspects into the identified boxes on the grid so that you can see the full team profile.

Focus on the aspects that are towards the top left of the grid as shown in Figure 6. These are the priority areas of development for the team.

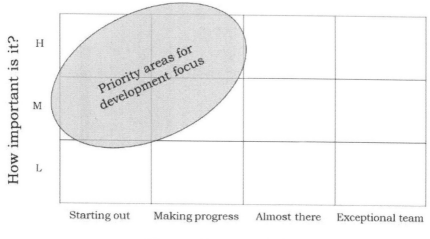

How well do we do it now?

Figure 6. Priority Exceptional Team Blueprint areas for development focus.

This prioritisation activity could be carried out in a number of ways. The chosen approach will depend on the time available, the team situation, the ease of getting the full team together and the level of engagement desired. Some options are given below.

- The team leader carries out the assessment and decides on the priority development areas themselves. They then present their view to the team for discussion and seek engagement and involvement to refine the outcome.

- Each team member does the activity individually and then reviews the overall results. A discussion is facilitated to reach consensus on the team development priorities.

- Team members pick the top three aspects they individually think are the ones that need development. The level of consistency of views across the team is reviewed, discussed and the priorities agreed.

- A full team activity is facilitated to reach consensus on the priority of each aspect in turn.

Once the priority areas of development are identified, work through the following steps for each area.

1. What are the potential solutions that would address the priority development needs?

2. What resources and support are needed to deliver the solutions? Resources include time, money, support or advice. This helps to make sure that the solutions identified are viable. It also helps the planning of when, and how, to deliver them.

3. What are the success criteria for each solution? How will we know that development has been achieved successfully?

4. What are the timescales to complete each development solution? This will give focus and allow a plan to be produced to manage time and activities effectively.

5. Start to implement the chosen solutions!

Identifying priority development areas - Key learning points

- Don't try to work on every aspect at once – unless it's a new team that's just starting up.
- Focus initially on the key areas that will make the biggest difference and have the largest impact on the team's performance.
- Use an appropriate approach to populate a prioritisation grid to decide which of the aspects to focus on.
- Consider the importance of each aspect in terms of driving the performance of the team forwards. Make sure you cover the future direction.
- Consider the current capability of the team against each aspect.
- Position all the aspects into the identified boxes on the prioritisation grid so that you can see the full team profile.
- Focus on the aspects that are towards the top left of the grid. These are the priority areas of development for the team.
- For each priority aspect consider the potential solutions, resources required, success criteria and timescales in order to develop them.
- Implement the solutions.

My Plans, Reflections, Ideas, Next steps and Thoughts

Acknowledgements

I owe huge thanks to the following people for giving their time to contribute to this book and helping to validate the Exceptional Team Blueprint™. They are great people involved in some great businesses and organisations.

Mark Averill, 'Av It! Media
Craig Barker, koobr
James Blake, Talk Staff Group
Julie Broad, Rolls-Royce plc
Simon Bucknall, EMBS
Sean Clare, Blue Arrow Derby
Bev Crighton, University of Derby
Karen Cureton, Cureton Consulting
Jon Eno, Hot House Music Schools
Stephen Goddard, KuKu Creative
Yvonne Gorman, Essential Print Services
David Hyner, Stretch Development
Diz Lamb, Ardagh Group
Paul Naylor, Direct Help & Advice
Lucy Rennie, LR Comms
Graham Schuhmacher MBE, Rolls-Royce plc
Sharon Stevens-Cash, Gravity Digital
Terry Stock, Rolls-Royce plc
Amanda Strong, Mercia Image Print
David Torrington, Sky Recruitment Solutions
Rob Twells, Frogspark

Meet the author – Andrew Deighton

I'm an Employee Development and Human Resources professional with significant development, change, talent management and senior HR experience. This was developed by working for Rolls-Royce plc for 26 years in roles across the Aerospace, Naval and Commercial Marine, Submarines, Civil Nuclear and Operations sectors as well as in corporate positions.

After an initial career as an engineer, I've led the HR workstream on a £40m manufacturing facility build, I've been a Head of Employee Development and the Head of Early Career Pipeline. I've had international experience as the HR Director for a global division with over four years based in Singapore. I developed the executive recruitment, development, succession planning and reward strategy and processes for a three company joint venture team bidding for a £7bn nuclear decommissioning contract.

I'm a Fellow of the Chartered Institute of Personnel and Development, a Member of the Professional Speaking Association and have BPS Level A & B psychometric accreditation. I've a degree in Mechanical & Materials Engineering, and postgraduate diplomas in Engineering Business Management and in Human Resources Management.

I'm a voluntary mentor for students at the University of Derby, a Trustee of the DHA charity in Derby, and a volunteer with the Inspiring the Future organisation.

I set up AWD Development Solutions Ltd. in 2014.

The Exceptional Team Blueprint™

I hope you've found the Exceptional Team Blueprint™ workbook useful, worked through the activities and started to make progress on developing your team.

To enhance and supplement the learning from the book, I run workshops and Masterclasses which go into much more depth. They allow time to identify and focus on your team's specific priority development areas.

I offer consultancy on a project or retained basis to review where your teams are and to implement the interventions needed to make your teams, your team members and your leaders exceptional. I can facilitate your team meetings to make them more effective and efficient. I can design and run your team away events.

I coach individuals to help them become highly effective team members or leaders using the Exceptional Team Blueprint principles. I can also provide team coaching.

I deliver talks and keynotes based on the elements from the Exceptional Team Blueprint to networking groups, conferences and seminars.

Get in touch to discuss how I could help you to improve the performance of your business or organisation using the Exceptional Team Blueprint™ approach.

Email me at **andrew@exceptionalteamblueprint.com**

Follow me on twitter at **@xteamblueprint** and connect on LinkedIn at **linkedin.com/in/andrewdeighton**

And check out **www.exceptionalteamblueprint.com**

My Plans, Reflections, Ideas, Next steps and Thoughts

My Plans, Reflections, Ideas, Next steps and Thoughts

My Plans, Reflections, Ideas, Next steps and Thoughts

My Plans, Reflections, Ideas, Next steps and Thoughts

Printed in Poland
by Amazon Fulfillment
Poland Sp. z o.o., Wrocław

54722528R00152